PEN &

PULSE

ESSAYS ON WRITING, CRAFT, AND THE WRITER'S JOURNEY

ESSAYS BY JENNIFER CLARK, JOHN BISCELLO, KELLI ALLEN, ANDY SMART, TAYLOR GARCIA, ALIA LURIA, JOSH RANK, BROOK BHAGAT, LINDA CARADINE, DAVID NASH, TYLER JAMES RUSSELL, AND MICK BENNETT

EDITED BY SUMMER STEWART

CONTENTS

CRACKING COLLARBONE JONES

BROOK BHAGAT

When I saw it, we had been in bed for days in my little rented room in Poona, just up the road from the ashram. We'd miss morning meditation, miss afternoon meditation, miss the parties, and then run out to eat at a 30-rupee thali kitchen before they closed. The lilies I'd given you the first night had dropped their petals on the concrete shelf by the bed, leaving their naked stems in the wine bottle vase. I was awake, watching you, your long eyes, your nose, your full lips, your mouth, slightly open as you slept. I touched a faded scar on your cheek and your eyes opened.

*****

I first saw Bernini's *Ecstasy of Saint Teresa* in an oversized hardcover I was supposed to be reshelving at my work-study job in the art history library. It captivated me: the aching angle of her marble neck, hidden beneath frozen robes; her mouth, falling open; her eyes, rolling back under fluttering lashes in the ether of god-pleasure-pain. I made mine of clay, no model, just my desperate imagination fleshing out a man in the same posture, on the same line between worlds: not Jesus, but long-haired, bearded. Not Buddha, but with generous, tender earlobes. It was a bust, shoulders and collarbone to crown. In my head, I called him Collarbone Jones for his gaunt clavicle, wrenching forward as his head fell back in rapture.

He was the embodiment of my secret wish, of what I was looking for in India. I had no words for it, but that invisible, wordless desire was so important that I saw no point in making any other plans for my life after Vassar. When anyone asked what I intended to do after graduation, all I could do was mumble, "work somewhere and save up to go to India." If a "why" followed, I'd shrug or say I didn't know, but that was a lie. I knew what I was looking for: that ecstasy, that look on the face of Saint Teresa.

I didn't want to talk about it, but I had to define it, if only for myself. Sculpting it was an act of both defiant hope and dark desperation—I had a hateful doubt, a bitter inkling that it did not exist. That I was chasing pipedreams and make-believe stories of old Zen masters from my Eastern Religion class and library books that looked like no one had ever checked them out but me. That I was destined to come home empty, as empty as when I left. Who would dare say out loud that she must find Enlightenment, must find the Divine or die trying because a life of jobs and apartments and minutes flapping by was just a slow death without it? Sculpting my reason, my need, made India all or nothing, heaven or hell—I would find it or I wouldn't. Putting a face on what I was after meant admitting I was risking everything, meant it was possible to fail, but it didn't matter. Nothing mattered anymore.

A numb pointlessness had permeated my life, a dull depression. My passionate ambitions for writing and art and New York looked stupid now, useless. What would great literary success buy? A covering for the hollow bitterness that gnawed at me like a cancer, like frostbite in my gut? I found myself with nothing to say to my friends, nothing to do but go through the motions, drifting to classes on campus and drifting back to my apartment like a ghost. From my mattress on the floor, I started each morning looking out the window. If it was sunny, I might go to class. If it was cloudy, I went back to sleep. It's cloudy a lot in New York.

As a senior art student, I had my own key to the sculpture studio. I made nothing else that last spring, dragging Collarbone Jones out over the whole semester. I skipped sculpture class half the time, preferring to work on him at night. I'd go around two in the morning, and if the glass walls of the studio were dark, that meant I was alone. Before going in, I'd pull a cigarette from my hoody pocket, sit in the dirt near the trees, and watch my reflection smoke in the yellow light of the lamppost.

Inside with the fluorescent lights on, artist's rituals followed. He rested on a three-legged wooden stand, high enough to put us face to face. Wheel him slowly to the center of the room, away from the crowd of sculptures in the corner. Take off the thick, once-clear plastic, now muddy gray with slip. Walk around him, touch his cold cheek. Drag my fingers over the rivulets of wavy hair. Spray down the face, the back, the shoulders. Decide what to tackle: more definition for the hair? Fix the Cupid's bow? Make the lips cracked, or smooth? More hurt in the brow, drawn up in the middle, or more pleasure?

My favorite tools and sponges were stashed on the far counter, under a pile of forgotten smocks. Over endless nights and hours, I learned new ways to get what I wanted. Half-dried clay, pressed on the jaw and ripped off, made a rough beard. The eyes would remain empty, but I could build eyelids, half-closed like the saint's, if they were thin enough and I could hold them on, blowing on them until they dried enough to stick. I wet my thumbs, cupping his cheekbones and smoothing his temples with slip.

He was also alive, of course. He was everything I wanted to dare to believe in. With him, alone at night in the studio, I could feel things again: I cried pulling up the lines of the forehead, cried holding open the mouth. I kissed him once on his hard clay lips, savoring the fine gray grit on my tongue.

One night, going to refill my coffee can of water, I tripped on the spindly leg of the stand and it flipped in a second, no way to catch it. I see it now in slow motion: how I screamed, like seeing someone get hit by a car. How I rushed to him, kneeling, how I couldn't breathe, how my heart banged in my chest—but he was okay. He had landed on his right cheekbone, almost unharmed. How I fell back, sat on the cold marble floor with my elbows on my knees and my palms on my forehead. He was okay.

I couldn't get the cheeks to match again, though. No matter how I built and blended, the right side remained flatter than the other side after the accident.

One day, he had to be finished. The semester was ending, the show was coming. The endless always ends. I didn't eat the day he went off to the kiln for fear that he would crack, and he did—a magnificent hairline fracture wandering back from the corner of the mouth, a thin line branching straight down from the corner of the eye like a tear. I loved him more for breaking.

*****

A year later, watching you sleep on the other side of the world, I couldn't believe I hadn't seen it before: the full lips, the nose, the beard, the long eyes, no longer hollow. The cold, gray abstraction of meaning come to life—warm and brown and breathing gently. I touched your cheek.

Your eyes opened. "What's wrong?"

"What happened here?"

"A motorcycle accident a long time ago. This cheek is flatter. But why are you shaking? What is it?"

"It's you."

HOW TO MAKE YOUR FAMILY PROUD (OR HATE YOU) WRITING ABOUT FAMILY

TAYLOR GARCÍA

PART 1: THE SUBJECT OF FAMILIES

Let's first start with the general idea of what a family is. We're each born into one. Most of us come from a nuclear family, which starts with a mother and father, however nuclear families come in all varieties. Some of us come from single parents, or parents of the same gender, or blended families, which include stepparents. Some of us were raised by aunts or uncles, or grandparents. Some of us have large nuclear families, while some of us are single children.

For some of us, our extended families play a big role and are very present in our lives, while some of us may have very little exposure to our extended families. Some of us were raised by a family friend, or have a network of friends that feel like family. This is the world into which we are born. This is the stage upon which we are placed. More on this concept later.

Then, as time goes on, we make friends, and assemble friend groups who become like family. We also begin our romantic and sexual lives, which leads to finding our partners and oftentimes, our spouses, which in turn often creates a new family. We continue this process of building networks of family units our entire lives. A good example of this is our work families, or the various social communities we belong to outside of our blood families. You're probably part of a team where you rely on a few people to share in your collective work. Some of these people you might like or dislike, some you might even love.

Whatever the size, shape, or make up of the various family units in your life, you are part of one, whether you were assigned to it or you chose it. And you also have very private feelings about those people in your family networks. After all, these groups of people support, nurture, and sometimes abuse us, and we reciprocate accordingly.

What I can say to that is: it's okay to have those feelings. You can love someone in one of your family units, then hate them the next day, and vice-versa. This is all very human, and you should keep feeling this way.

So, why families as a topic or subject to write about?

First, we can all relate to it. The concept of family is universal. Because we each come from one, we are all equipped to reflect and comment on ours. Families are near and dear to me because mine, both my birth/nuclear and extended families were everything to me when I was younger.

PART 2: THE FAMILY AS A STAGE

When I was quite young, I made up a saying: "The family is the stage on which we learn how to act." Pretty smart, huh?

Sure, it's not a new concept. Modeling has long been the explanation for just about everything in the field of child psychology. It's why we say, "Monkey see, monkey do." I am, in fact, living in a real-time child psych laboratory where my two sons under ten imitate my every move and word—the good stuff *and* the bad stuff.

My early grasp of family as a behavior incubator comes from my upbringing in a small dysfunctional nuclear family surrounded by two very large and spirited extended, and also dysfunctional families. (Did I just tell the story of your life?)

Layered over that family structure was our cultural and geographic influences: Southwest Hispanic Americans of Mexican, Spanish, and Native American descent steeped in Catholicism, all within a 300-mile radius in central and northern New Mexico. We've been isolated, landlocked, and tightly networked across a few smallish cities and towns for literally hundreds of years. *Como dice el dicho: pueblo chico, chisme grande* (As the saying goes: Small town, big gossip).

Growing up, weekends were filled with birthday parties, First Communions, baptisms, weddings, funerals, etc. During junior high and high school, I attended a wedding—or was in the wedding party itself—at least once every other month for all my older cousins. Holidays involved huge gatherings with lots of food, music, drinking, dancing, and games. Basically, any reason was a reason to be together, and that meant a celebration.

My nuclear family gravitated more toward my father's animated and dramatic side of the family, where I had most of this non-stop celebratory exposure, due in part, to the dysfunction in my nuclear family. Dad wasn't fond of Mom's side of the family, and he preferred to be with his family of birth versus our own nuclear family.

My mother's side tended to be more earnest and at times, stoic. There were certainly dramas and scandals and characters on her side of the family, but they were less "publicized" and frankly, my sisters and I didn't have much exposure to mom's side because we were always defaulting to our dad's side. Regardless of the side, those cultural and religious influences weighed heavily, and informed much of who we were when they were all together. Therein is the key observation I made, and continue to make, about that family stage I mentioned earlier: I had three stages where I could watch comedy, tragedy, and melodrama, and therefore had three stages upon which I learned to act.

Fast forward to now, and the matriarchs on both sides of the family are long gone. The individual families have broken off into sub-groupings. The dramas of the past have left scars too deep, and thus divisions and alliances have formed, and new dramas and scandals and characters have developed. But it all seems to be eroding in such a way that makes those tight bonds we once had seem less significant with the passing years. We are truly in the last season of this telenovela.

So that's a bit about my family, and it's the reason I write about the subject. It's the stage on which we learn how to act, where we experience our most joyous and painful moments. And there's just such great material!

PART 3: SO WHEN AND HOW DOES IT GET TOO PERSONAL?

Anyone here know who Steve Almond is? He's the author of numerous books, essays, and short stories. He was my workshop leader at the 2007 Tin House Summer Writers Workshop, when I was in my writing infancy, and I have been madly in love with him ever since.

In his short book, *This Won't Take But a Minute Honey* (which I highly recommend), he comments that when students ask him what they should write about, he responds with: "Anything you cannot dispose of by any other means."

If you have to get something off your chest and you can't do therapy for whatever reason, writing is the way! So, give yourself permission and do it, and know that it will get personal. You will doubt whether to do it, but you will let go of a lot of baggage. You will grow, forgive, mourn, move on, and celebrate.

So what to let go of?

All of it.

So, why is it important to do it?

Someone out there will pick up your book or poem one day and they will automatically relate to what you've written. They too have experienced the same thing, or you have written it in such a way, that they feel exactly what you were feeling. That's the therapeutic process for you and the reader (and your family). This is the very essence of mercy and compassion; it's what Steve teaches and what he says we, and all of our characters, deserve.

By choosing to write about family, you're giving you and your characters and situations (your old memories about your family) mercy, and who doesn't deserve a little mercy???

PART 4: HOW TO DO IT (PHILOSOPHICAL & TECHNICAL)

I've talked about why you should do it. Now the how.

Short answer: Any way you goddamn want to. Seriously.

You're going to be writing about real people. It's going to get messy. Accept that. If you're a fiction writer, you can disguise, obfuscate, embellish. It all works. Poems, you can do whatever the fuck you want anyway. But in any case, you're writing about one thing, and that's a moment in time about a person near, and sometimes dear to you.

You're writing about that "one time," or that one tick or trick or trait that you loved or hated. You're writing about the sweetest or scariest moments, or those people you adored or abhorred. It's up to you to change the details of the character and settings, or make them extremely real.

Consider for a moment some of the teachings of Joseph Campbell. Campbell, as you probably know was an American writer and professor who theorized what's referred to as the monomyth. It's a sort of template or unified theory for heroic narratives. Essentially, the protagonist leaves an ordinary or known world for a special or unknown world and is transformed along the way.

Now consider a story or memoir you're writing about family. Your protagonist is on that same hero's journey. As a writer, you are moving your central character (or in most cases, you) from the world of the family (the ordinary) and into the strange and dangerous places away from said family. Or, this could even happen within the context of a family. For example: kid believes his parents are happy, but finds out that his dad works for the CIA and his mother is a serial killer and just a matter of time before everything changes. That's ordinary to scary and the hero didn't even have to leave home.

As you begin to write specifically about family, you begin to home in on those moments, those secrets, pain points, traumas, and what-have-you, which your hero is carrying with them into a new world. Everything else you write is simply a support system for those precious or terrifying moments.

In short, Campbell's hero's journey is the quintessential trope for stories about families. As you begin to plot out that story inside of you, think of your central character as the hero. They have to move from here to there in order to have redemption, in order to dispose of what they cannot rid themselves of by any other means.

Here are some things I bet you cannot dispose of by any other means:

- Your true feelings (good or bad) for a particular family member
- Your degree of love or ambivalence toward a family member
- How you are drawn to or repelled by a family member
- Power struggles within a family
- Family members living with different agendas
- The fight for attention
- Unsaid feelings
- Dysfunction as function

- Love circles, triangles, squares, trapezoids (yes, these all exist)

So, these are exactly what you should be writing about.

My short story collection, *Functional Families*, is, you guessed it, about families. Mostly my dysfunctional family. In some of the stories, I chose to write directly about someone in my family, while in others I used more composite sketches or archetypal character traits.

EXAMPLES FROM MY STORIES INCLUDE:

- BIRD DOG:
    - o REAL THING: estranged relationship with my father and his true identity
    - o How I adapted it: Based the aged, advanced dementia father on a distant elderly cousin my family used to care for, used her living situation as the basis for the father character, used real elements of my father's life to incorporate into the story
- BAT OUT OF HELL:
    - o REAL THING: an often-mean-spirited aunt and her recurring tall tales

- o How I adapted it: Created a close version of this aunt but made her a grandmother figure, amplified her actions and behaviors, focused on how they affected her children

- MONICA IN GEORGETOWN and SAD LAST DAYS:
  - o REAL THING: mother-son co-dependency trope
  - o How I adapted it: Used sketches of moments with my own mother, and other mother/son relationships in my family, examined and satirized the little king stereotype that is common in Latino mother/son relationships

IN CONCLUSION

When writing about family, you are going to be inhabiting the psyches of people very close to you. You're going to be living their realities, and that is going to be dangerous and scary and weird. You're going to be digging up old memories and traumas, which is also terrifying and probably forbidden. But, if you're willing to do the work, you'll receive a first-hand lesson in empathy, catharsis, and redemption (for both you and your subjects) in the most beautifully creepy way you can imagine. That's what writing is anyway. It's just part of the job.

Writing about family showed me that we all have things left unsaid or unresolved tensions, and we have to let go of those somehow. We all deserve closure for bad *and* good things. It's the only thing that allows us to move ahead in our hero's journey.

One other thing: Heroes are themselves transparent, and transparency is so hot right now. Jump on that. Disclose. Say it up front. Being transparent with your readers is a good thing: either in a preface, opening pages, wherever; it's okay to share what and who your work is about. Especially if it's about your family. I did this at my book launch party, which, of course, was mostly attended by my family. I said, "You may find yourself in these pages!" (So far, no one has come forward with a death threat.)

Lastly, do you need permission to write about *your* family? No.

And besides, if they're an astute reader (of if they're brave enough to actually read your book), they'll figure out it's about them.

Suggested Reading about families:

Snow, by Dorianne Laux (poem)

There There, by Tommy Orange (novel)

GUIDE TO BUYING, SERVING, AND STORING REJECTION

JENNIFER CLARK

I. Buying

Take your pick.

There are many fine rejections out there. Connoisseurs will speak of good years,

great years, and seasons which range from unexceptionally grapey to vaguely flawed.

Here's a sampling:

2023. I'm going to have to pass on writing a blurb, however, having taken the resolve to quit encomiums for the foreseeable future because I've too much on my schedule that is due or overdue. Time gets so precious the older we get. Someone told me it's like a roll of toilet paper — the nearer the end, the faster it turns. Oh well.

2018. It came close.

2014. One great and two rather pleasing rejections go down easy.

2012. Though an excellent year for prose, the rest is a bit more uneven.

2011. Complex, worth savoring. (Get drunk on Pushcart.)

2010. Much "isn't suitable."

2009. Buzzes with rare, handwritten notes in a swarm of *we have to pass*.

Remember: it's the ones who never even taste your work that sting most.

Passing is part of the game.

I wrote a poem about basketball that wasn't rejected. In fact, it got slapped with an honorable mention by a team of judges. Speaking of which, one of the greatest basketball players of all time, Michael Jordan, by his own count, missed more than 9,000 shots in his career. *I've failed over and over and over. And that is why I succeed.*

It helps to know you are in the company of giants.

(Note to self: Write more basketball poems. Maybe dedicate one to M.J.)

II. Serving

Right now. Somewhere.

Fine work is being rejected. Mine. Probably yours, too.

Decant rejection into a clear glass for further inspection.

Taste is subjective. However, make it a habit to pour rebuffs of any kind into a clear stemmed glass. Heat of hand transference may be avoided by holding the stem. Swirl the blunt notes. Sniff. Really get your nose in there. You can't always tell just by looking if you harvested words and served them before fully peaked. Rinse well. Repeat.

While these steps may not necessarily modify your palate, it may influence how you develop future flavors. For instance, you might learn that cinnamon doesn't need to be sprinkled into everything.

Do not regret to inform others.

You will fight with your spouse over what to put in the annual Christmas letter.

People don't want to hear about failure, the spouse will say. Failure is not festive.

Point out that people weary from hearing only good news. Don't give up. You will win.

From your generous stock, pull out your most hearty rejection; pair it with humor for loved ones far away: *Her most recent poem was rejected with great enthusiasm as* "unfortunately it does not evince the heavy sonic texture (alliteration, rhyme, assonance, consonance)" *that the editor was looking for.*

III. Storing

Heat and lack of oxygen are the enemies of success.

So that your craft does not grow stale and flat, keep putting yourself out there. When We Regret to Inform You arrives, repeat this handy ditty: *Fresh rejections flowing means the grapes are growing.*

The important thing is to breathe deeply and keep writing.

Store rejections in a cool place.

Do not stand them upright in a hot, dry room. Avoid those who store their nays thusly, like the writer who approaches you at a coffee shop and demands to know what you are writing.

Do not breathe in as you look into their eyes which resemble two drops of harsh tannins. Repress the urge to say, *Fuck off.* It is a small town so instead reply, *An essay on rejection.*

While you aren't each other's biggest fans, you admire the way their poems have a tendency to sprout sharp teeth. One even bit an editor who accepted their poem and passed on yours. Admit editor made the right decision. Your poem only nicked the surface. Their poem, though harsh and verging on cruel, clung way better and left you bleeding.

I've got a much better topic for you, they say, their face flushed. *Writer envy. Write about that!* A grin explodes across their face, as if they have just blown the cork off the writing world.

Not familiar with it.

You should be. It's out there. This town is crawling with it.

Recalling this encounter years later, take a deep breath. Recognize you can share the same pond yet stand on different shores.

It bears mention again…cellar rejections carefully.

Take heart; editors must decline worthy works, some, believe it or not, even more worthy than your own. Editors are generally well-mannered and wish you much success with your writing and hope you keep them in mind. They may remind you that they, too, are writers. Be gentle with them. Procure what morsels they toss your way. All will be lost if improperly stored.

Keep records.

Rejections are like stones skipping across a pond.

One skip. Another lone skip and then two skips along with a scrawled note: *there is evocative prose here but …*

Three skips. We admired its inventiveness, but in the end, the story wasn't a good fit for us.

Four skips, impossibly almost there. Your piece was the subject of spirited conversation among our editorial staff. Your prose is simple and understated. Ultimately, we decided not to accept the piece for publication.

Be glad they skip at all.

Remember the first sip.

It is a sunny day when you march two blocks to the corner of Inkster and Park.

The creaky yawn of the metal mouthed mailbox swallows the manuscript destined to change the world. Inspired by Allan Jaffee's *Funny Jokes and Foxy Riddles,*

you've spent the summer of '75 toiling over *Humor My Mother Doesn't Appreciate.*

The day the letter arrives, it is raining. Or maybe it is sunny. You will only remember standing in the kitchen, your father watching as you rip open the envelope addressed to you. Turns out, like your mother, Penguin Books, or maybe it is Putnam, doesn't appreciate your humor either. A kindly refusal is typed on letterhead with a bird or a moon or both at the top. Smudged in the left corner margin, along with your hopes, is a handwritten note: *Keep writing!*

You realize the world (a.k.a. one person hunched over their Smith-Corona in New York City) has not been waiting for such a book. You are too young to realize that a personal message is golden and should be savored. However, you are old enough to know that how you handle this stone is how you will handle the hundreds of stones yet to dash their way across your heart. You stand still as a pond and do not cry.

OPENING A DOOR AT THE CLOSE

KELLI ALLEN

When traveling, we come upon a new shore and must remember the story of Faithful John. One companion may protect us from the seduction of the New, may even turn to stone so our chests are not burned through to the thick lungs despite our vest of silver threads clutched tight over bone and sinew. Another might gather our wrist in his long fingers and pull back toward the receding waves. We follow both too often, leaving John to mind a horse head weighing-down the rucksack containing language, fastening against a way home.

So many stories begin with "long ago," "once upon a time," and "there was…" Our experiences are a snake eating her own tail, yes, but recollection in words is not just agreeing that ends and beginnings are sometimes inseparable, it's tucking the tail's tip deep into our throat. No matter how far we wander, our bodies return to the same familiar hut and say *here is your tundra, here is your Slavic forest. How will you again leave and enter? Through the door, the window, the stove's narrow pipe?*

Storytelling is sometimes about luck-casting—it manifests in the hope that the gathered listener will find their way in, and bound by empathy, hunger for the questions too long tied to a young captain's mast. What other practice has such fine regard for the ether and weft of chance, of the squidgy ash-brows that line capital K-knowledge's garden paths? Story opens us to risk fault and fury, kinks in the skein, and ultimately, it allows us the great leap from intention into fruition. But these are wispy imaginings, still free from acknowledging what ends, what stops, what forces heel to ground and toe to badger den.

Why do we pay such particular attention to the way in which a story concludes? The high school language arts instructor insists that we care about endings because of basic neurocognitive focus, which underpins one of the prime concepts in rhetoric - the most important parts of a speech are the beginning and ending, the castle and the dragon. The value of primacy and recency declares that when we put down a book, we are later likely to remember being caught up and swept along rivers of opening lines and brought to some worthy muddy bank by the last. Consider clichés we ascribe to the experience of being taken into a great book from the first, how we felt when at last it ended, but in the pages between we have only a sense of momentum.

Our tales beg for closure more than our bodies during the adventures and observations fueling the craft. Readers care about last lines in particular. In poems of course, usually in novels, but also in lives doing some living - we gift a name to what brackets a life: the epitaph. We recount the (most likely apocryphal) last words of notable persons to give them a summation, a sense that their last moment was a comment on all the moments before (Emily Dickinson, "The fog is rising"), or a counterbalancing, sad commentary on the lengths they'd fallen from former heights: "Rosebud", or Nietzsche's asking after a horse. The most important part of a joke is how it ends - the punch line (e.g. Socrates' last words - "I drank what?"); without it, the joke has no action, and without a worthy one, no humor. In drama, there is sober reflection on evils done, or the sweetness of redemption that gives weight to all the suffering before as more than sordid wallowing in pain. Two examples of last lines, which grip the reader for both their finality and their circular reflections, are from Nabokov's *Lolita* and Wally Lamb's *I Know This Much is True*:

"And this is the only immortality you and I may share, my Lolita." (Nabokov)

"This much, at least, I've figured out. I know this much is true." (Lamb)

In both of these instances, the reader is brought back to the beginning of the text while at the same time reminded of the work's title which allows for a circularity and closure that do not imply a specific definition of emotion. Rather, the text relies on itself for closure and makes certain that the story requires the reader to decide of its ending value instead of neatly telling whether happy/sad/ambiguous are necessary labels. This is where we watch Faithful John stand in his corner and nod, not twice, but once.

Our visual stories are granted no immunity from addiction to ending. As in our own videos—the perfect vacation, staged heroics overcast by a storm, an infant clutching a sweet in her fat fist—how often do films get re-shot after test screenings, changing the ending because the audience was not satisfied? With complex middles, like tipping a scale closer to senility, or the teen committing to journey from his nest, it takes a robust momentum - or multiplicity of character, or sublime simplicity of character - to offset that balancing ballast. Think how the film "Return of the King" had as many as seven separate endings, just to hedge against an unsatisfying conclusion to the epic trilogy. Or how Neil Gaiman's *Stardust* broke with tradition by ending not with a wedding and the cheat of "happily ever...", expected of fantasy romances, but through a mortal ending until an immortal stood in loneliness, as Arwen after Aragorn, to a different kind of never-ending.

For many cultures across many timelines a story's ending seems inevitable, foreshadowed and built up until it has the force of nature, like a great pendulum swung all of one way in preparation. People find comfort in form, know what to expect, and are disconcerted if an author breaks with form by way of experiment or commentary or contrariness. But this contradiction and surprise can also be the entrance of sublimity. Think of the "re-written" conclusion to the story-within-the-story of the screenplay "Stranger Than Fiction" where the author's great, seminal work is undone (literarily) by giving Harold Crick a different outcome, collapsing the metastory and choosing life over artifice. His life stops being a pedestrian character study of someone trapped in patterns of habit and numeracy when the unfeeling universe, unprepared to reward his attempts to change anew, but meant to show the shallowness of all life as arbitrary, runs him down by that most hoary of philosophical harbingers of death, the Bus. Yet, because he accepts his fate as written, voluntarily stepping into the way of Bus, he is in fact reborn, redeemed. When Faithful John becomes stone, he does so because the story's demands are ancient and set. Drama is not just the patter of rain on black umbrellas around a grave plot. We can see this in Gabriel Garcia Marquez's *One Hundred Years of Solitude:*

Before reaching the final line, however, he had already understood that he would never leave that room, for it was foreseen that the city of mirrors (or mirages) would be wiped out by the wind and exiled from the memory of men at the precise moment when Aureliano Babilonia would finish deciphering the parchments, and that everything written on them was unrepeatable since time immemorial and forever more, because races condemned to one hundred years of solitude did not have a second opportunity on earth. (Marquez)

If we return to our places of solitude, garments folded onto shelves, John asleep beside our bed, we are making room, too, for Chekhov.

Anton Chekhov defied endings in every conventional sense known to fiction of his time and prior. He removed himself completely from the Aristotelian plot wherein devices were constructed to demonstrate and create catharsis with a text's ending. Chekhov employed a subversive tactic in his fiction that left, and leaves, many readers with a sensation that the story is somehow incomplete. His endings allow stories to move into realms of anti-epilogue and reverse epilogues. The implication here is that by focusing on the past near a story's end, the future is essentially denied—change will not occur, thus disallowing for a tied-with-a-bow ending. Remember a time in your wandering wherein the expectation for succor and ease was replaced, from a shadow behind, by confusion and peril? Surprise does not equal finality, rather it screams *next!*

We crave climax, the cathartic exhale constructed for our memory's pillow tops. But digesting a text is every reader's burden, and every writer's tease. Perhaps, then, both the surprise and the zero endings are just an aesthetic reaction to an excessive formalism, just as impressionism responded to realism in painting, as atonalism did in music, and as did much of modernism. The ship navigates its waters as expected, the Nafs in our bellies revolt, and the ship becomes a swan. If "dénouement" is the French for "untying the knot," then a surprise ending is like Alexander the Great cutting the Gordian Knot (boldly breaking with convention), and the zero ending is like a frayed but intact knot remaining after fruitless effort. It is the same when the Queen falsely grieves her son's death, and the King deals new cards for every jester locked in their damp cells.

We think we are safe, and we arrive near the final door. The initial excitement in reaching for the brass knob is followed by the inevitable, "and now?" Surpassing the classical didactic ending of the myth or fable and morality play, the challenge of the surprise or non-ending raises the unbounded question of what is possible. If a dramatic trajectory goes from an arc to an abrupt turn (surprise), to stopping at an arbitrary point (zero), perhaps to an ellipse (the implied but unstated end), to a circle (ouroboros), to a dashed inconstant line (stream of consciousness), or even the streaks of lines, whorls, and clutter that is Joyce, where pauses our hand? Perhaps this leap into uncertainty underlies why we feel disquiet and bothered when unexpected ending are sprung upon us, for we have been seduced, riled up, brought to peak and then...diverted, denied our happy ending. Just as the last line of Margaret Atwood's *A Handmaiden's Tale* brushes the hair out of our blinking eyes: "Are there any questions?"

Not all of Carthage shies from zero ending, or from the lovers bent away from union. Should it be a comfort that for every *Pride and Prejudice* there are more of *Catcher in the Rye, Gone With the Wind, 1984*, and *Hunchback of Notre Dame?* Even where there is some measure of redemption, an ending like Ian McEwan's *Atonement* is more about what could not be undone. Or like the tragedy of *Romeo & Juliet,* where in the end, the only solace is to learn from events and, with death, sue for peace among feuding families. That dissonance resonates within our breast, a thrumming low and pained, and perhaps it lasts longer and leaves marks deeper than that sweet trill of happy reconciliation we've been conditioned to crave. Why else would art so often be lauded for its detailing the dark instead of the light? Just so, we are cloaked in speculation and miss the crow's baubles entirely, so we must circle back.

Faithful John steps forward each time we sigh in relief that an end is clear, is certain and clean. He reminds us that no rest comes until what we hold most dear is sacrificed—over and over. Have we agreed to so much hubris that we can ignore his warning and instead walk to a celebration we never intended to design?

The teachers will always arrive, will encircle us while we are drunk and lost. They will seal the bourbon cask shut and force us to grope through bound pages, excavating only one layer at a time.

Where we shine a flame to frame the poison dart in our pocket is the middle, end, and beginning of each story we allow.

REVISION AS A CONVERSATION

ANDY SMART

For years I hated revising. I equated it with the proofreading I learned in high school and conflated revising with revisiting what I learned in that Lutheran institute. It was, I felt, eliminating such grammatical errors as dangling participles and misplaced modifiers. Death to violations of subject-verb agreement. Punctuation! Never use exclamation points. I have failed the ghost of Mr. Reiss already. Apart from being an academic exercise, I looked at revision as an imposition both in the sense of requiring time and effort that could be spent on something else and insofar as everything done in the process of revising was done *to* the work. As a student I had been taught. As a writer, I took a blank page and put words on it. I wrestled those words into phrases and sentences, pushed blocks of sentences together into paragraphs according to the rules I learned, and that was that. If everything worked and the copy was clean, revision was over. But, of course, I was wrong.

Revision is not the one-sided affair I once believed it to be. It's a conversation.

I confess I came to this conclusion by way of literary pretentiousness: studying theory. In the gap years between my bachelor's and grad school I went through a dark-glasses-wearing phase of ultra-serious intellectualism. By this I mean I read well beyond my purview and well past my depth. I couldn't even pretend to hold my own with philosophy, so I took on Terry Eagleton's *Introduction to Literary Theory*. From there, my curiosity somehow led me to an excerpt from Rita Felski's *The Limits of Critique*. Therein I encountered a term I'd never seen, heard, read, thought, or dreamt of: *dialogic*.

In Felski's essay dialogic is treated as a buzzword, neither a praising adjective nor a pejorative. But as the essay progresses dialog becomes increasingly sweeping in its scope. First the work is in dialog with its contemporaneous works—the writing of an era is talking to the readers and writers and books and poems and stories of that era—but also with the works that came decades or centuries before. Felski argues that context, in the narrow sense of taking only the meaning which is imparted to a written work by its immediate historical circumstances, is an injustice not only to the work but to the reader and the world in which that reader moves.

Let me back up.

I was rejected by the Iowa Writers Workshop and Washington University in Saint Louis when I first applied for my MFA in creative writing. I limped into David Clewell's office, an attic toy store full of alien paraphernalia and first editions and cried. I literally cried and I'm not ashamed. Clewell, however, the crusty old greybeard that he was, barked:

"So they say you're not good enough. Who the fuck are they?"

Clewell was my friend and mentor at Webster University where I finally, at age thirty, finished my undergraduate degree. He was a former Poet Laureate of Missouri, a friend of Philip Levine and James Schuyler, and a chain-smoking doppelganger of Walt Whitman. I loved him then and I love him now.

"They're the people who know," I said.

"Get the fuck out of here."

"What?"

"You have to ask yourself if you really believe that. If you really believe that they are the arbiters of what's good, of what's right, of your value as a writer. Ask yourself that."

"Well—"

"Not now, not here. Get the hell out of here and go have a serious conversation with yourself."

For the first time, I was confronted with the notion that academic authorities were not necessarily infallible. Maybe, if I decided, I could live without their endorsement.

I went back to the poems and the essay I had submitted to the programs who rejected me. Were they my best? Were they things, as William Carlos Williams would have called them, I was willing to hang my hat on? They were not. I had submitted work that felt like it had been written and I was disappointed in it. I was disappointed in myself.

When I told Clewell of my newfound perspective he asked the inevitable question:

"What are you going to do about it?"

Revise. Try again. Go back to the desk and do better.

Revision became a conversation with myself. What do I want? What do I mean? How do I want to structure this thing that I'm crafting?

From there it became a full-fledged reinvention of how I talked to myself. As I typed the new versions of old poetry I would ask out loud *Is this a poem?* Every sentence in a prose piece was subjected to a round of intrapersonal doubts: *Why is that capitalized? What is the overriding sentiment? Are you absolutely sure you need to say this?*

Revision is a conversation between the writer and the writer. We are, as Phillip Lopate assays, not fully ourselves on the page. We necessarily create a persona with enough distance and perspective to write about the hardest things in our lives. The narrator, speaker, or main character in our work may be us, but it's the version of us that we negotiate with our own wellbeing and our own writerly sensibilities.

Where do our sensibilities, tendencies, fondnesses, strong suits, weaknesses, and insatiable curiosities come from? How many of you flinched at a sentence ending with a preposition? Why?

Because we are also in constant conversation with those voices of our past which first put me off revision: teachers, tutors, hand-me-down maxims about not writing like we speak, and so forth. Those voices, however, can't be allowed to do all the talking. As writers we must be willing to argue with them. We must at least maintain a healthy distrust of their absolute authority. Rita Felski decries this type of skepticism, saying it thwarts our ability to read without critiquing—critique being a passe fossil from bygone days of academia—but I disagree. Skepticism can and possibly should fuel a writer's relationship with language.

Consider the word itself: revision. Resee, re-*en*vision, imagine in multiple ways. Instead of simply going back to the work and performing a face lift to make it look like Strunk and White, show it some photos and let it decide. Put some makeup on it and have a look together. If something about your writing feels off, spend time with it. If you've created something that produces friction with your hardwiring, ask yourself why and how. More importantly, ask the work.

Let me back up.

In January of 2018 I finally found an academic home at the Solstice Creative Writing MFA program at Lasell University, a handful of miles outside Boston. I was part of a seven-person cohort of nonfiction writers who would spend five two-week residencies workshopping one another's manuscripts, with the end product being a 150-ish page creative thesis. In the second half of that first residency I met Anne-Marie Oomen, a Michigan farm girl whose authorial accolades could fill the Oceana County phone book. She was our faculty facilitator for five days and she began with these instructions:

"When you talk about one of your peer's work, refer to the voice on the page as The Narrator. It's not personal, loves. As we discuss each manuscript we will go around the table three times and everyone—except the writer—will speak.

The first time we will simply make observations: *I notice this narrator says 'y'all,'* for instance, or that the narrative is fragmented, or that every sentence has the same number of syllables. The second time we will speak to any issues of clarification: are we unsure who is telling the story, are we confused as to where we are in time as the piece moves along, and so forth. The third round is what I call the Love Fest. This is where we celebrate the things we personally liked or were touched by.

After that, we'll open it up to a group discussion that will include the writer and we'll make suggestions for revision. Any questions?"

"Anne-Marie," I said, "what are we supposed to do while we're being workshopped?"

"Take notes, listen. Remove your ego from the equation and consider what your colleagues have to say. Once you've heard them out and had a conversation, take the manuscript and interrogate it."

"Interrogate the manuscript?"

No one can elicit an *-ly* adverb from me like Anne-Marie. Observe:

She smiled knowingly.

"It will make sense in time, dear heart."

As we followed Anne-Marie's template for our craft debates it became clear what she meant. Innumerable times one of us would say something like *this piece feels like it wants something else.* Manuscripts came alive and started making demands. Give this one more scene work and less narration; this one is super lyrical, let it be a prose poem; this wants to make the reader feel anxious so take out the commas and let the text do almost a stream of consciousness thing where nothing can stop it unless the text decides it's time.

And so I learned to talk with, not to, my own creative work.

The last piece of business at residency was mentor assignment. We had to choose from a list of three possible faculty members with whom we would swap creative and critical work for the following semester.

"Looks like you and me kiddo," Anne-Marie said.

"Lookin forward to it," I said.

For the next fourteen weeks she and I emailed fat batches of fresh, critiqued, and revised pages from what would become my first book. Attached to every packet exchange was a cover letter, a prose summation of what was going on in the manuscript and in our lives. When I sent a packet to her, Anne-Marie always emailed me a confirmation that she'd gotten it and would be reading it soon. Her responses were elegant, voluminous, and insightful; she helped me braid together the parts of myself I had thrown into my work and helped me pull in parts I was afraid to. I confessed my trepidations and my foibles. Told her all about the imposter syndrome running rampant in my head and the binge drinking I did to combat it.

"You worry me," she said.

"I'm fine, just fine," I replied.

"You're such a man sometimes and your book is very masculine. I love you both but it's something to consider."

"You mean revise the writer as well as the writing?"

"Something like that."

Revision came to mean, alongside dialogs with myself and the work, the conversations I had with her. The ways I began to see myself as a writer, the ways I approached my work, what I elected to read. These all reflected the relationship I had with my mentor. For a moment this epiphany—Anne-Marie insists on epiphanies in nonfiction, so this is for her—made me uneasy, even disappointed. I had consciously rebelled against professorial authority and now I found myself deeply indebted to a new mentor. I was letting her steer me on and off the page and enjoying it. What was different now?

My engagement. Anne-Marie taught but didn't pontificate. Recommended but didn't prescribe. I couple perceive an impact on her by the end of our first semester together (there would be a second one when I composed a tediously pretentious critical treatise on Roland Barthes and writing mental illness; Anne-Marie's revisionary guidance is the only way I survived that project. I suspect wine helped her).

Revising is a conversation with other people. I'd talked with my friends in shop.

I had a testy exchange with the editor of a (now defunct) online literary journal following a rejection of a submission of mine.

I smoked countless menthol cigarettes on my front porch while my best friend from high school and I poopooed the great Russian novelists and spent the untold millions we would doubtlessly make as the future avant-garde of American lit. What did we know? What did we know about writing and it's crowded lonely offices?

But the biggest difference now is the people I talk to.

Anne-Marie is family now. I trust her with anything. My buddy Mark, too. He wasn't in my cohort but in the fiction group who set up shop in a conference room upstairs from us.

We started chatting about George Saunders on a sofa in the common are of the dorms and texting two or three times a year; by graduation I would have lain in traffic for him and I still would. Somewhere in the D.C. metropolitan area a ferocious essayist friend is revising her marriage and drafting what will be a bestselling memoir. All I need from her is a head nod at a given phrase and I know I'm cooking with fire; her first two publications were in places I told her to submit. All three of the aforementioned writers are unafraid to tell me I've made a mess of something or to hear me do the same for them.

Our conversations, mine and my brood of confidants, are revision.

In *Dead Poets Society* Robin Williams asks his students about the purpose of language. The first response is *to communicate.*

"Wrong!" Williams says. Language exists to seduce other people. Far be it for me to disagree with the late comedic genius, but instead I'll offer my own revised version of his thesis: language exists to be shared. The story of humanity and its evolution is full of languages and examples of their usage to share, to witness, to proclaim. All these acts are dialogic; they all commune with the past, present, and posterity. Language is a human experience, connective and communal even in its myriad dialects and variations. When we invoke language to express an idea or even to seduce someone, we enter a discourse with forever.

In this sense, reading is a conversation. Writing is a conversation. Revision is a conversation.

THE PITS AND SEEDS

JOHN BISCELLO

True Artists Don't Starve. The romantic myth of the starving artist pricked and deflated by this statement which he had seen printed on a T-shirt, accompanied by the decal image of the "unstarving" artist: half-moon grin on his kisser, goblet in hand, upraised, eyes blazing a self-assured glint, a sense of triumph swelling his chest. True Artists Don't Starve.

He had seen the T-shirt sported by a young, bespectacled man, several years back, and the young man had sat next to him on the front porch bench at the Cup, his regular coffeeshop haunt. He had asked the young man, pointing at his chest: What exactly does that mean?—and the young man had smiled and answered—We've got to destroy the old myths. This, and he pointed to the phrase on his chest, is about a clean break from tired conventions. At the time, he had liked the young man's answer, liked the energy with which he had spoken it. Destroy the old myths, a clean break from tired conventions. Like he was saying: Why be a penniless poor sap bleeding romance from dried-up flowers, when there was a whole garden endowed with bounty and abundance. This phrase, this T-shirt, was flag-worn by this young man as an emblematic fuck-you against the Poison Rose of self-consciously cultivated suffering. A Poison Rose is a rose is a rose … so trample the fucker underfoot and grow some new flowers.

Yes, at the time, he was heartened by this young man and his T-shirt, thought that it spoke high-volume about new possibilities and re-defined conventions—tomorrow was but a postcard away—and now, if he saw that young man, that T-shirt, he'd spare no violence in tearing the flag from his body, and stuffing it past bloody gums down his throat till he choked on it, force-fed every letter and implication of his precious ethic.

The heat through the coffee cup warmed his hand, the other hand stuffed into the pocket of his trench-coat. He looked out at the snowcapped mountain, the rest of its dense body tinted blue and gray. He had been in this high desert mountain town for over five years, and everything—the good, the bad, the ugly—circled back to the Mountain, the ultimate alibi and scapegoat, the power-source which mafia-commandeered the whole goddamned town. He wanted to be childish and defiant, so he hissed fuck-you to the Mountain, knowing it was blameless, yet also knowing it could take it. Kick and spit and swear at the Mountain, it didn't matter: the matriarch, impassive and unflinching. Like the greatest of mothers, or goddesses, you'd like to believe the Mountain understood your source of frustration and anxiety, and would not admonish, but go on understanding, endlessly. It didn't matter if it were true, he liked to think that.

He would go to the bank soon. Tess had loaned him $300, and after giving his ex- wife, Elle, $100, for child support, and the purchase of coffee and last night's drinks, he has $190 in his pocket. Plus the $100 check he had gotten as a Christmas bonus. He had gotten the bonus on Christmas Eve, and it was only a week later, when he had decided to stop showing up for work. No phone call, no explanation, he just stopped showing up. One day, you have a job, and you report to that job on a regularly scheduled basis, this is part of your program, not necessarily Life, but part of your program, then one day you decide to throw a monkey-wrench into the program, just short-circuit the whole thing with a seemingly random act of sabotage. Seemingly random, yet there was a fastidious and cunning build-up of calculation to the whole thing, wasn't there? It came in the form of a sudden and unexpected explosion, but the bomb-makers had been secretly counting the ticks all along, hadn't they?

All together, he had $290, plus $150 in the bank, which brought his grand total to $440, still $110 short on rent. That was last month's rent, and this month's rent was due yesterday. Walking back home, thinking about all his eggs in one basket, and the basket was rusty and coming unhinged, and the eggs were cracked, running yolk, yet he kept going and going, thinking about this intensely as he walked: Was this the solid flame of conviction or a fool's delusion? Time, in its passing, would tell. Even though it was bitter-cold, no more than ten degrees, it felt good to be walking, it reminded him that he was solidly upon the earth, being of mass and substance: connected.

Halfway home, mulling possibilities for cash: call up Joe, the editor of the ski magazine, whom he had freelanced before in the past, three times the past year. The articles paid

$150 a pop, and never took very long. Note: call Joe. Then there was Willy, the publisher of the local alternative newspaper with a socio-political slant. Willy had hooked him up with freelance jobs in the past, and even though they had had their disagreements (both he and Willy were temperamental fuckers), the rifts were usually short-lived, water under the bridge, and Willy had never refused to throw a bone his way. Note: Joe and Willy. Who else?

Almost home. His friend, the Professor, Lucas Archnell, was on break from his teaching post in Costa Rica, and in town. Lucas had hit him off with loans in the past, and as a gay man, enjoyed having his straight friend, kept, by leash of economy. If you don't pay me back one of these days soon . . . we'll have to find other ways for you even the debt. If he called him up, threw a little of the ol' charm around, flirted mercilessly, maybe he could procure another small amount. In the least, Archnell would offer to take him out for drinks, so there was something to be gained.

Home. His tiny casita, bordered by a Spanish Baptist Church, and his neighbor's enormous house. He loved this place dearly, and the idea of possibly losing it, if he couldn't come up with rent money, was very disheartening. The intimacy of its dimensions, allowed him to see everything, save for the bathroom, in one panoramic scan, an enclave whose parameters inspired warmth and comfort. Where the limits of space left off, the Imagination began. So, following that turn of logic: the smaller, or more contained the space, the greater the expanse in which the Imagination could move. Concentrated, contained: that's what he loved about his house. He checked his machine to see if his landlady had called. Click. Voice of a robot: One new message. Click. Voice of a different robot: This is an attempt to collect a debt, if you are—

He unplugged the phone. He sat down on his brown recliner, and tried staring out blankly, but it quickly led back in, so he got up and went to his fridge and opened it. A carton of eggs, four left. He would use two right now, and two for breakfast. He had eggs, hardboiled, for breakfast, now it was dinner, and to avoid monotony, he decided to make egg salad.

He set the eggs to boil, then looked in the fridge again, and pulled out a Tupperware jar set in the back of the fridge. He had forgotten about the bread his ex-wife, Elle, had baked for him a couple of weeks ago. He opened the plastic lid and took out a misshapen chunk of sourdough. To test its density, he knocked on it several times: rock-solid. He turned on the oven, placed the bread on the bottom grill, and closed the door.

Time seemed to be moving both faster and slower these days, and if only he could stop it, just a little, the briefest of pauses in the great scheme of movement. Time. Stillness. Breathing. More breathing. Water boiling, gurgling. He turned off the flame, and everything, eclipsed, continued. There are many things which happen in life, dramatic and un, and dramatic only because of contextual definition of–this is, was, dramatic—as such, and many things happen and many things don't happen, non and un, and yes and no, and right now what is happening, a still-life, in motion, for the records: There is a young man tapping the shell of a hard-boiled egg with the back of a spoon, and when the shell cracks, he begins to peel off the shell, the whole if it, piece by piece. He repeats this action in unshelling a second egg. Both eggs are placed in a bowl, and he uses the back of the spoon to mash up the eggs, and when they are sufficiently mashed, he adds, with the same spoon, a glob of mayo, and dollop of ranch dressing, then proceeds to mash the eggs, mayo, and ranch all together, finishing the procedure with a generous sprinkling of salt and pepper. That is, was, Life . . . anything else is a fine-sounding Lie, the succubus- sister in a knockout dress.

No, he wasn't starving, nowhere near starving—and to pretend otherwise would have been a grave insult to those who were really starving, yet . . . hunger. There had always been this hunger: monstrous and unappeasable. Spiritual, mental, emotional, whatever its origins, this hunger had split into a hydra-headed beast with each head compelled by autonomous demands. To be fed, to consume. Like a rampant infection, it spread throughout the body, a wildfire scorching a drought-dry landscape.

The library: a refuge, the safest of harbors. He had always felt that nothing bad could ever happen at the library, that he was safeguarded against the evils of the world. Like, when you are a kid, and you're playing tag, and you run around like mad, trying to avoid being tagged, and there was the respite of *base*, that place where you went, and were exempted from "getting caught." A refuge, the safest of harbors.

There he was: scanning the shelves with quiet intensity, the names of writers, living and dead, dreams recorded and catalogued in rows of books, inspiring the burn and itch of speculation: would his name one day be among these names, was there a shelf-life in store for him?

Again, the hunger. Words upon a page, the reading of books, a distinct form of eating, digestion. He would ravenously consume print and chew and swallow whole paragraphs, pauses, periods: each ingredient with its own distinctive taste and seasoning—paprika, colon, thyme, oregano, semicolon, garlic, ellipsis, parsley, implication. Hunger, yes, but he was certain he would never go hungry so long as libraries functioned as restaurants with a full menu of books to eat. Hunger—and he found himself in the H section— Hamsun, and the book he had written in the late 19th century, *Hunger*, and recalling the protagonist who at one point, in a fit of delirium and hunger, viciously bit into his own finger, craving the taste of flesh and blood: his own. Then, there was Chaplin's hunger in the *Gold Rush*, boiling his boot in a soup for supper. Both of these examples spoke to, and underscored his own hunger, neither seemed far-fetched or obscene in any way: Eating your own finger was as good as eating your own boot was as good as anything else when it came addressing an insatiable hunger, a hunger more about one's own state of being than their body and its groan-volumed needs.

And today's take-out order: *The Chauvinist* by Toshio Mori, *The Magic-Maker*, a biography on e.e. cummings, *Little Disturbances* by Grace Paley, and *Twice-Told Tales* by Nathaniel Hawthorne. He checked out his books and left.

He began reading the collection of stories, *The Chauvinist*, by Mori, and was pleased to find, as was stated in the preface, that William Saroyan, at the height of his own literary fame, had "discovered" the work of Mori in a magazine, and lauded him with praise. And after reading several Mori stories, he could see why Saroyan would have been a fan: the casualness, and diamond-sharp simplicity of the style was reminiscent of Saroyan. For Saroyan, no slouch when it came to self-aggrandizement, it must have been like looking into a mirror and seeing a double-reflection. Mori's writing, like Saroyan's, possessed that unpretentious grace, and ground-down, salt-of-the-earth substance which Saroyan so greatly admired. Something clean and songlike: a fledgling bird and its innate conviction of flight.

When he got to the story, "Confessions of an Unknown Writer," he zipped through it breathlessly, than quickly re-read it again. After a second reading he closed the book and let the story sink in, settle. It had been the same way when he had read Saroyan's short story collection, *The Daring Young Man on the Flying Trapeze*—story after story raining blows to the brain, vigorous love-taps inducing shortness of mind-breaths, until he was dizzy and blissfully woozy: lost and found all at once.

Now it had come again: the unsuspecting and open reader caught off-guard by the quiet squall of song summoned by this man, this writer, Mori, whom, several hours earlier, he had never heard of. He opened the book again, went back to the story, and copied one of its passages, the one which had almost brought him to tears, into his blue spiral notebook. "I am back in my little room writing the end of this piece and thinking about myself, the writer. I am settled back and comfortable. I do not need to hurry. My head is clearer and I am returning consciously to the glare of a clean white paper before me. I become smaller and the size of the blank white sheet grows bigger. I become panicky and then dull. The silence of my room which is usually very dear to me begins to irritate me. All I have is myself, I think, and to commune with a clean sheet of paper is the costliest time of my life. I have no place to go, and I have nobody waiting for me. I am a fool, I am a big fool, I think to myself. I am wasting my life on nothing, and like a fool, will continue wasting it forever. For something to do I rush up to the mirror and look at my face. The biggest little sap, the biggest little sap, I keep saying to myself. What have I done in the past, and what shall be my future? I look at my old face and become sad. I think of my mother and her patience, and her belief in me. This is terrible. This is tragedy. I put the mirror down and look at the familiar objects. My old desk with scattered papers, the old magazines, second-hand books, an old typewriter, and the bare yellow walls. I walk up and down the little room until I become exhausted. Dimly I hear the train whistle, and the trains roar by. It is three in the morning, I think to myself. I sit down in the only seat I have in the room before my typewriter. Then, as I sit for minutes or perhaps hours, it becomes natural for me to sit before the typewriter and face the challenge of a white paper and life. Only then, I realize, I will sit and write even if I should become a fool. I will go on writing for life no matter that may happen for a few mad hours or days, that being a fool will not stop one from becoming what nature intended him to be."

Is that how time passes, he wondered, one eye scanning the digital red numbers on the clock. 7:01. Watching, watching, watching, stillness, breathing, being, watching, watching, waiting, waiting, beating: 7:02. Was that it? A minute born, a minute dissolved, a minute born, a minute dissolved: and slowly, very slowly, your body grew old, your organs grew faulty, your blood salty, your eyes weaker, teeth looser. Minute by minute: a corpse understudying your life . . . knowing one day its time would come.

Mori made him think of time, and time circled back to Saroyan, as he got out his old notebook, the one in which he recorded quotes and passages, and sought out the passage from Saroyan's story, "Myself Upon the Earth." When he found it, he read it aloud, in a voice loud enough voice for every literary ghost, living and dead, to hear:

"Furiously, I am smoking a cigarette, for the moment is one of great importance to me, and therefore of great importance to everyone. I am about to place language, my language, upon a clean sheet of paper, and I am trembling. It is so much a responsibility to be a user of words. I do not want to say the wrong thing. I do not want to be clever. I am horribly afraid of this. I have never been clever in life, and now that I have come to a labor more magnificent than living itself, I do not want to utter a single false word. For months I have been telling myself, you must be humble. Above all things you must be humble. I am determined not to lose my character. I am a storyteller, and I have but a single story, the story of man on earth. I want to tell this simple story in my own way, forgetting the rules of rhetoric, the tricks of composition."

He closed his notebook and pondered: Mori, the room, solitude, storytelling, Saroyan, time. Then he went to his desk, turned on the lamp, removed a red, spiral-bound notebook from his drawer, and set it on the desk. Debts, unemployment, unpaid rent, all of it would disappear if he could start a story and lose himself in it. With Saroyan and Mori in his corner, he felt confident he could do just that.

POSTSCRIPT TO A LIFE IN RUINS

LINDA CARADINE

In my new memoir, *Lying Down with Dogs* (Unsolicited Press, April 2024), I wrote about the difficulties I had at work and the eventual implosion of my 25-year career. At the time it was happening, and even a decade later when I was writing about it, I didn't know just how to attribute my failings. I didn't know how or why my once manageable professional life had turned into a shit storm of massive proportions.

Somehow it didn't occur to me that there might be some physiological cause for my sudden inability to function at a high level. Instead, I chalked it all up to simple burnout, an evolving disinterest in my field or, perhaps closest to the actual reason, some sort of generalized depression. While I was living through it, I believed I was no longer capable of doing my job. Granted, it was a demanding role. I was responsible for hiring and firing people, coming up with improved processes and, at the bottom line, ensuring the company made more money every quarter. Anyone, so challenged, might come to doubt their abilities at some turn. But I knew something was seriously wrong. I just couldn't quite put my finger on it. So I plodded on, disappointed and unsure of myself.

One would suppose that writing the book ought to have been a more intuitive and therapeutic process. And perhaps it would have been had I been describing someone else. The fact is, what happened was all the inevitable consequence to an entire life spent forgetting, procrastinating, dithering and tuning out. I knew I wasn't stupid. But, for the life of me, I just couldn't perform adequately. So, while obscuring the issue at work, I wrote about it in essays, diaries, stories and, finally, in my memoir. And there, when taken as a part of the whole of my adult life, a light came on. But I still didn't quite have the answer. I sought counseling in the hope that that would eventually jog some insight into my apathy, fogginess or disinterestedness. Whatever it was.

Instead, my therapist dropped a bombshell on me in the form of a new diagnosis.

Have you guessed it yet? In addition to depression and anxiety, it seems I have AD/HD. And that simple addition to my mental stew was a game-changer. I was able to receive appropriate counseling and medication and, suddenly, I was in charge of my own destiny again. At work and at home, I got my mojo back.

Along the way, I learned that girls and women manifest this disorder in their own ways and that our symptoms weren't always initially attributed to ADHD. After all, that's a disorder of hyperactive little boys who can't sit still in class, right? Who thinks an accomplished woman in her fifties would have it? I wasn't outwardly hyperactive or disruptive. I didn't act out. My mind didn't race with ideas and urges. Usually. I was just a spaced-out woman who didn't have the mental wherewithal to perform my job. I had a daughter to raise, animals to care for and my writing to accomplish. And my job was just something I did to get paid at the end of each month. I wasn't able to prioritize it or give it my full attention. Once I was effectively treated, that switch was finally flipped and I recognized the importance of doing well at work. Unfortunately, it was too late for my career. That particular ship had sailed. I'd done too much damage to my record and my reputation. So instead of continuing to spin my wheels, I decided to take early retirement and concentrate instead on those things that brough me pleasure.

I'm still writing about it, still pondering the ramifications of being "this way." But now I'm doing it from a place of knowledge and insight rather than one of guilt and frustration. Now I am able to better understand how my brain works. And I'm able to capitalize on my strengths. I can see the wisdom of being "differently abled" rather than disabled. Because, without a doubt, my condition comes with its own superpowers. I have the ability to concentrate on one thing at a time and to block out all extraneous thoughts. I am energetic and I am creative. I am resilient as well as self-aware. I maintain a positive attitude. I am a good communicator. These are all characteristics that I treasure.

Thinking back to my childhood, I can recall being a daydreamer and termed a "sensitive child" to whom tears came too easily. I was isolated in my own mind. Without many friends or goals or a knack for self-determination, I gravitated toward an all-consuming love of animals as many lonely girls do. I was forever stopping to pet them, adore them and bring them home. And that propensity, thankfully, has never left me.

I wound up starting a dog rescue organization and, in the wake of my ruined career, I was able to run it with that fierce fuel of unbridled passion. The rescue was a tremendous success and I wound up saving a lot of animals and making a lot of people happy. That, and my writing, have sustained me.

I have written and published dozens of essays, magazine articles and a couple of books. These pursuits bring me fulfillment. I am never bored. There is always a project afoot. There is always accomplishment to seek and pleasure to be felt. I write my life chapter after chapter and I am fully engaged as never before.

Friends have come into my life by virtue of my renewed interest in humanity, my own and that of others. My worldly pursuits have opened the door to connecting with other people who also love animals, who also write, or who also have an interest in the thousand and one other things that occupy my mind these days. I've learned that I am not shy or anti-social as I was led to believe in my earlier life. I just avoided people and new experiences because they overwhelmed me. I was always in self-protective mode, always trying to shield myself from being overrun with feelings, facts and ideas.

Now, when I think back to my pre-diagnosis life, it's a testament to sheer tenacity that I was able to achieve anything at all. I write about it all in pages and pages of careful prose yada-yada-yada and I think each time that I have captured it fully and correctly. But there is always more to say and another point to touch on. My disorder, for better or worse, has given me the ability to reach further.

Surely, I am convinced, there are other people like me. Undiagnosed neurodivergents who labor under the weight of some little-understood condition. They are perfectly average, or even great, adults who through no fault of their own have failed to thrive. For them, I wish answers. I hope that they will seek the holy grail of self-discovery that I happened upon by accident under the care of a perceptive therapist. You know if something is not right. Don't wait until circumstances conspire against you to bring havoc to your well-ordered life. You can get your mojo back. This you must believe.

Now I am almost seventy. I'm becoming an old lady. And I have always prided myself on letting go of regrets. But, damn, I wish I had it all to do over again. I wish I had steered myself toward higher education. I wish I had sought to be luckier in love. I wish I could have been more of a resource for my daughter who is kind and bright and perceptive but is similarly unfocused. I wish I could have lived a fuller life.

But I find myself here now. There is still time to redeem myself, still time to excel at the things I care about and to connect with the people I love. There is still time to live my true destiny. Everything that came before was just a bump in that twisty road that we all travel together. What's next, I wonder? What will happen today and tomorrow and for the rest of my days? Although my memoir has been completed and published, I can now appreciate the fact that it reflects just a chapter of my life and not the totality of who I am. I am still finding my voice, still writing my story.

WHY WRITE?

DAVID NASH

All I hear is

the blaring siren of doubt.

The odds are slim.

What's the point?

Who's going to read it?

What if no one reads it?

If no one reads it, what's the point?

You suck.

That was stupid.

I can't fucking write dialog.

No one says that.

Show don't tell.

Tell me more.

Cut this.

This doesn't work.

Not enough here.

You can cut this too.

Not needed.

Implied.

I'm sure there's a home for this,

just not here.

Why did you write this?

Why write?

When I talk to other authors, I realize I've had an interesting relationship with books during my first forty years. I don't remember when I started reading, but I recall my mom flipping the pages of "Alexander and the Terrible, No Good, Horrible, No Good Day" when I was feeling blue. I can see my dad nodding off as he paged through "The Indian in the Cupboard" while I stared out the window in my bedroom above the garage. I remember listening to my "Little Thinker Tapes" in bed and drifting off in the hazy, July nights of my Minnesota youth. In second grade, I lied about how many books I read so I could earn enough stars for the free Pizza Hut pizza offered through the school reading program. And late at night, beneath the covers, I freaked myself out in sixth grade as I read about a man's stomach getting sliced open by a resurrected dinosaur in Jurassic Park. His entrails practically slid through my fingers just like they did for the blinded Dennis Nedry.

When I got to seventh grade, I scored relatively well on an English literacy test. It said my reading level was that of a tenth or eleventh grader. A savant I was not, but when I saw that score, I pretty much figured I'd checked that box and would never need to put effort into reading again. I was set. Reading was easy. I was a genius. Later gator.

However, when I got to tenth grade, a similar test showed me I had (predictably) stalled at the stagnant comprehension level of an eighth grader. Shame and embarrassment pushed me to reluctantly try to read a bit more. I started with Harry Potter and flirted with Stephen King. It was great, but, still, I skimmed the Cliffs Notes anytime I was assigned to read in high school. The classics? I still haven't read most of them. I listened to a few, but often it goes over my head, and I end up daydreaming while the words float by. I did read "All the Pretty Horses" by Cormac McCarthy this summer after he died. It was beautiful.

In late high school, something shifted when I started trying to write my own songs. Even now, poetry has remained difficult for me, but songwriting was something I could wrap my head around. When the lyrics failed or became insanely cliche (soaring eagles, bleeding hearts, tears filling oceans… yuck), at least I could convey my thoughts by the way I slowly strummed the guitar or belted out a chorus. It was the first time I found joy in artistically creating something. I've been writing songs since I was fifteen years old, and twenty-five years later, I can't stop. It feels wonderful to write music. Ten to one, the songs are total crap. But when you find the tenth which carries all the right words and rings like Amazing Grace in your soul it feels soooo good. And when you start to share your songs and one finally connects with another person… Damn, that feels even better. They tap their feet and sway side-to-side. Maybe the audience even closes their eyes, which sounds cheesy, but whatever. You did that. It's awesome.

Still, in the dark corner of the noisy bars and coffee shops lurks the silhouette of a monster. A hungry beast with fetid breath and jaundiced eyes: Imposter Syndrome. It's waiting to show its gaunt face during the long silences after the last chord rings out when no-one applauds. It pops up when a kid half your age performs a brand new tune that they "just wrote that day" which is so phenomenal, it makes you want to sell your guitar and curl up in a heap on the sticky bathroom floor of a subway station. That creature definitely whispered doubts in my ear when I sat down to write my first book.

In a breathy, steaming voice, it leaned in from behind the old orange chair that sits in the corner of my bedroom.

"Who do you think you are trying to be a writer? What do *you* have to add to the literary canon? Nothing," it says, shoving the answer down my throat. "You have nothing to add, and you can't write worth shit."

There is always a part of me that believes the beast, because the truth is, I never set out to be a writer. Not even once was it in the plans. When I did decide to write that first book, I think

I got extremely lucky with the two-word response that popped into my head.

When those doubts flooded in, I naively thought "why not?"

That's it. I didn't flinch. I just started typing. I didn't think about publishing. I didn't think about book sales or movie rights (still waiting on both of those). I didn't have friends cheering me on until later in the game. My wife raised her eyebrows if that counts as affirmation. I had no Rachel Hollis' telling me to shoot past the Milky Way with my dream-board goals. All I wanted to know was what the story would look like, so I asked myself "What if Paul Bunyan was a real person and his tale was more sad than the silly cartoons made it out to be?" I was curious. I poured two-fingers of whisky and started clicking away.

Before I knew it, I had a novel in my hands. *I wrote a book.* I'm skipping a few details here, but that really was about it. Of course, I had to pause for a moment to search the internet like a rookie for things like "how many words are in a novel" and "how to publish a book." Then I had to edit the shit out of the thing before it found a home. But one day, I woke up a published author. It was like morphing into a different species overnight. Wouldn't you think that would be enough to silence that shrouded character in the shadows throwing skepticism my way? I wrote a book, damn it! Don't I deserve to be here?

Yet, the question continues to surface like a rising trout picking off mayflies.

Why should I write?

When I ask google how many people have ever lived, it tells me 117 billion people have been born, give or take. With that many humans having spent time on this planet, I'm pretty sure I'll never have an original idea. Whatever story I write, it's been done before or told at a bar or yarned across a campfire or stuttered in the hull of some rickety old ship as it lurches and rocks its way across the ocean.

So why the hell should I even start on my next big idea?

What's the point?

That's when the little cricket hops on my shoulder and speaks two powerful words. The same words that crept up and silenced the Imposter Syndrome that one night a few years back.

Why not?

Really. Why *not* write?

It's fun.

Sure, it's work.

But the act of creating is just… Fun.

And if there have been 117 billion people, and, unless we kill the planet in the next fifty years, there will likely be another 117 billion, the odds are that just ONE of those folks is feeling the same things I was feeling when I wrote down my story. One person has likely gone through the same emotions as my characters. And it's just as possible they didn't have the time or space or ability to express it. Just maybe, my words, *your words*, might resonate with them. If you have the chance to connect with someone on that emotional level, your writing is worth it. And you know what? If it doesn't connect with anyone, who cares? At least you did it. Nothing is in vain. That piece of trash you wrote a year ago might have been cathartic as it helped you process the betrayal of a friend. Maybe it got you out of writer's block. Maybe it cleared space for a new storyline. Maybe it spun a web that leads you to a better idea when the morning comes as the single strand leads in a surprising direction glistens with morning dew. Or maybe you revisit it and realize your character dialog was racist and shouldn't be shared with anyone and thank God you've now learned about some of your unconscious biases.

Do I still hear that awful, doubting voice in the creaking floorboards of my quiet house? Forever and always. Even as I write this essay, that voice creeps up. *Who am I* to share thoughts on writing with you? The topic of writing has already been covered by many more accomplished and learned authors. You could read Anne Lamott (I haven't read it), Ray Bradburry (haven't read it either), Stephen King (listened to it), Benjamin Percy (I did read that one), or Ursula Le Guin (haven't read it). There is a trove of literature and youtube videos and masterclasses out there to guide you through the thicket of your writer's journey.

But you know what, I DID write this one, and you've never heard of me before.

I'm a nobody.

But,

I'm a writer.

And you can be too.

You just have to *do it*.

So when inspiration strikes and the face of a hero interrupts your train of thought while you stock shelves, start an IV, fill out that spreadsheet, don't hesitate.

Write the story.

Afterall,

why not?

EMPATHY IN WRITING

MICK BENNETT

I always wanted to have a novel published. Why I didn't achieve the goal until the age of sixty-one is up for debate. Perhaps it was because my work lacked true empathy. It is one quality I believe novelists should cultivate. Whether it be through awareness or action, novelists need to wrestle with the emotional states of their characters, their neighbors, and even their country. The trick is to know your own emotions first.

For me, that self-knowledge encountered unexpected detours.

Beginning at age five, I was treated to yearly visits from our home in Belmar, New Jersey to New York City. My mother had modeled couture in the city just after high school. She knew downtown Manhattan the way I knew the arranged toy soldiers under my bed. On various trips she steered Dad and I to the Museum of Natural History, the top of the Empire State, and lunch near Rockefeller Center. Each visit was preceded by a visit to Dr. Goldberg's office, where a batch of chalky, choking barium was fixed up especially for me. I stood behind the fluoroscope and swallowed. And swallowed. And then went to see dinosaur bones.

At age nine I got a surprise. No chalky white stuff. Instead, I was informed a had a hole in my heart by a very nice doctor with a southern accent. He told me I had nice veins, and that I could call one friend and tell him I had a hole in my heart. My friend replied you can't live with a hole in your heart. Nevertheless, my hole was patched at New York Cornell Medical Center on April 4, 1962, and nine days later I came home. Pissed off.

It would get worse.

Back at school, told to avoid steps, I entered my elementary school on the girl's side of the building. Yes, the genders had their own sides—I can imagine a contemporary bigot bellowing, "There was no side for all of those letters!" I walked up the two flights of steps rather than the three on the boys' side and explained what I was doing and why to the rotating dozens of eighth-grade girls who had Hall Patrol duty. I took walks and listened to the principal console me as I wondered silently, *why not tell the hall patrol girls to stop harassing me*? I couldn't answer the kids' questions changing for gym class about my scar. *I don't know why it's on my right side...* I couldn't tell girls why I kept my shirt on at the beach. Too many questions without excuses for answers.

In eighth grade I noticed an add in the back of a comic book. I ordered a kit containing lessons on how to be a writer.

Weeks later a gentleman in a jacket and tie came to our house. He carried a briefcase with thick binders and spoke with an accent. My parents let him in and sent him up to my room—can you imagine that happening today? Dad called me in-house to tell me not to sign anything. The man left without a sale.

I have no idea what the hell I was thinking. Perhaps I needed to tell somebody my story.

They called it a post-graduate year. The masters at Blair Academy referred to me as a PG. Thirteenth grade I told myself. An extra year of high school for a late-blooming underachiever. But in my one year at Blair Academy, I fell in love with writing. A couple of wonderful teachers, interesting fiction, and factual texts. The American History texts, for example, were documented with scholarly articles and void of the colorized charts and old-world paintings of men wearing puffy collars signing documents by which few of them lived. I began to read for the love of reading.

First attempts at fiction were fun and awful. Fancying myself a playwright, I penned long winded dialogue just to see where it took me. Drama gave way to short fiction and angry essays. My four years at Gettysburg College, however, were dominated by social activities, sports participation, and insecurity, my constant companion since my adventures back in fourth grade. I lacked the courage to share any written work I wasn't forced to turn in for credit. Ingenuous and naïve, I married at the age of twenty-one in the summer of 1974 prior to my senior year. Nine days before Labor Day, I landed my first and last teaching job. I dove into American Lit, reread novels and stories, relearned grammar, and learned how to teach, all the while unaware of events back home in New Jersey.

My parents' health deteriorated in the two years after I graduated. My mother suffered a brain aneurysm from which she slowly recovered. My father wasn't as lucky. His cancer was inoperable and untreatable, and as plans for sale of my childhood home and final preparations were being made, I recalled a certain writer's storybook first novel.

F. Scott Fitzgerald, spurned by Zelda, his Southern Belle, went home to St. Paul, Minnesota and completed *This Side of Paradise*. Career established and Zelda won. I had the same hopes for my first novel, *We Were Stardust*. It was to be a journal of four young people during the summer of 1969 culminating in a visit to the Woodstock Arts and Music festival. Taking my title from a line from the song "Woodstock" by Joni Mitchell, I started writing in the spring after my father's diagnosis. Through the summer, into the fall, the handwritten manuscript—I couldn't type—grew taller and more soiled. I called bits of eraser between pages shit-page sandwiches. Pencil smears and smudges hid countless changes. That January my father passed; the book was far from finished. I put it away—the entire ridiculous notion seemed useless.

My marriage—rather predictively—wasn't prospering. We hung on for one more teaching year. Near the first anniversary of my father's death, I packed up my manuscript, found myself a consumptive eight-room motel two miles outside of town, and got back to *Stardust*. I wrote nights after coaching my ninth-grade basketball players, wrote in school during my free period and study hall duty. The novel took on dimensions far too complex for me to fathom at the time. It became part obsession and part excuse for the failure of my marriage. Both were finished that spring.

And I was still pissed off.

The remainder of my twenties was spent chasing. I didn't much care what or whom. As for my manuscript, after getting it typed, I learned I needed to have an agent. Between notching lifeguard saves on the beach and serving frozen drinks in bars on the East and West coasts, I mailed it out. It came back except for the one time it disappeared. I wrote more stories and began another novel. There would be three more, each weaker and less interesting than its predecessor. And then a girl whom I had taught in tenth grade walked into my bar back in Pennsylvania and ordered a Michelob. The following fall I was thirty, married, back teaching at my old high school, and back in graduate school, pissed off no more.

At Shippensburg University I had the great fortune to meet the poet John Taggart. His creative writing class forced me to share my work with other students. Their feedback was positive.

Soon I read works about which I had never heard: Stendahl's *The Red and the Black*, John Gardner's *Grendel*, William H. Gass' *The Pedersen Kid*. I met and spoke with Gass. I wrote Raymond Carver with questions about writing. In graduate-student relentlessness, I inquired if he possessed a tiny clock inside that told him it was time to end a story. He replied, "It's an interesting notion." My master's thesis became a collection of short fiction with an introduction detailing how Carver's fiction influenced my own.

John showed me how to send submissions out to literary magazines. Hand typed (single finger hunt and peck to this day), on good cotton fiber paper, with a cover letter, and SASE (always check if the publication requested *no paper clips, please*). How far down page one to begin the manuscript. How to edit. How to tuck the pages into the envelope—the right size envelope—so that when it was opened, the cover letter and manuscript would come right-end up and ready to read. My *Writer's Market* became my Bible. One day I received a rejection from *The Northwest Review* along with a comment regarding a previous submission. That previous submission became my first published story. I became fiction editor of Shippensburg's literary magazine and won the Mabel E Lindner award for creative writing. John guided my bike down the street, pushed me, and sent me on my way. I will always be grateful.

Still teaching at my original high school, I continued sending out stories to literary magazines. A typical story might take weeks to write and rewrite, then weeks to type. Frustration-wise, nothing compared to reaching the bottom of a page only to mistype a letter or misspell a word and begin a new page. For a mistype, out would come the correction tape—Wite-Out was considered careless by the unseen literary masters of these publications—and with luck, I could backspace and erase the incorrect letter and then type over it. A page every half hour became my average output.

Then to the post office to weigh my submission and purchase stamps for the original and SASE. *First Class* I would write on the envelope's back, along with *Do Not Bend.* And after sealing the envelope's clasp, the P.O. worker would drop my baby into the outgoing mail. The counting of weeks into months dragged like school the days before Christmas break. At times I had multiple submissions out and kept each magazine's suggested reply time on my submissions calendar. I became familiar with three types of rejections: receiving my manuscript back with the customary standard rejection slip, receiving a hand-written note encouraging other submissions, and the dreaded return of a thoroughly dog-eared, creased and fingerprint-smudged manuscript that would require a complete retyping. There was an art to these submissions, and art didn't recognize the Xerox machine.

Although my ambition to write long narrative fiction gave shorter fiction generous attention, John recognized—much sooner than I—that more formal training was needed. He suggested I get myself into an MFA program. I could become an adjunct to supply an income. I began looking around. A program at Temple University appeared promising, and John had a connection there with a former colleague. I hesitated. With a new marriage and new starter house, I didn't know if I were prepared for a new environment. John encouraged me to look into my wife's blue eyes and take the bold step. I paid my fee to take the GRE.

I showed up early the morning of the exams, placing a thermos of coffee and several sharpened pencils on the too-small desk. As the room gradually filled, I imagined myself teaching undergrads and living with my wife in a small walk-up somewhere just outside of Philly. Teaching undergrads, English majors, in an environment I knew would feel uncomfortable to my wife. I left those pencils on the desk for someone else's use and walked out of the room.

I have no regrets.

In time I developed the ability to instill empathy in my novel's characters without moralizing or preaching. They needed to be prepared to tell everything about themselves. They had to have one another's backs. A connection, a link to allow a longer tale to come full circle.

I learned that writers make their own world. Perhaps one of my favorite writers Raymond Carver put it best:

Every great, or even every very good writer, makes the world over according to his own specifications... It is the writer's particular and unmistakable signature on everything he writes. It is his world and no other.

My specifications probably relate to the boy in fourth grade getting over his anger and becoming more attuned to some other human being in a similar situation. In my writing experience, I've gone through cycles. For years I wrote nothing but novels. Rather than improve, they seemed to fall into a chasm of mediocrity. None other than *Stardust* ever saw an editor's or betta reader's eyes. Then I switched to short stories for two decades—perhaps too long a length of time to sustain real interest without continued success. With my teaching career heading toward retirement, I returned to novels. In the last two years, I've become attracted to shorter fiction—flash fiction to be exact.

There are advantages and disadvantages when your dream comes to fruition at the age of sixty-one. On the minus side, it comes as a surprise to most of your remaining friends. Your parents are no longer living. Your former teaching colleagues may be surprised or jealous. And there will always be the question of why so long? Why didn't you find success earlier? Hemingway said a writer "...has only been born with the ability to learn in a quicker ratio to the passage of time than other men..."

I was always a late bloomer.

The advantages? You'll never suffer through decades of inactivity. Death is a flawless excuse to not produce. No one will say, "He hasn't written anything of value since…" You can write what you damn well please and not concern yourself with what will sell and what agents are looking for. You will understand and not suffer any indignity when even your children and many of your friends buy your book with absolutely no intention of reading it. You might just have lots of fun.

I empathize with all of today's young fiction writers. Camus said, "Fiction is the lie through which we tell the truth." In American life today, it is hard to tell where lies begin and end. For that reason and others, books are not popular. America seems involved in a continuous dramatic spectacle which never resolves itself, and in which many treasure their chosen roles more than the wellbeing of their neighbors. At the height of the conflict in my new novel *Take the Lively Air*, a character muses:

The day's drama had dissolved into a hodgepodge of confusion and misunderstanding. Not a single line of reason appeared in its manuscript. Riley could only guess what drove the other players. He suspected their actions, as well as his, were molded by fear. Not a conscious fear—not a rational avoidance of danger—but pervasive, unreasoning fear of fellow players. Sensing the play's lack of direction bred mistrust and selfishness. Ad libs flourished, soliloquies were shouted, and the play fell

into a shambles, its finale in doubt. Even the audience sensed the production lacked a conscience.
Exeunt omnes. No curtain calls.

We all have much work to do.

MINING FOR STORY

TYLER JAMES RUSSELL

When I picture a writer starting *any* new draft, I imagine a prospector of some kind. Bend-backed and dirty, maybe in a canyon, or beside a riverbed. He is weary, determined, something McCarthy-esque about the whole thing. He wanders on, carrying a pickaxe or kind of awl. The point is: he's searching for something precious. Silver, maybe gold. Every so often, he drops to a knee and drives his tool into the earth, head bent, listening. But there's nothing to be heard. So he waggles it free and continues on.

Most of the time, this is all that happens. Sweat, dust, and emptiness. But once in a great while, our figure hears the deep, satisfying *thrum*—a vein deep under the earth.

As a writer, I often feel like I am discovering rather than creating, as if the story already exists either out in the world or latent in my brain and body, and my job is simply to stumble around until I find its borders. The point is, I tend to go by "feel" when it comes to deciding what to pursue in the earliest drafts of a story. I write until I feel that *thrum*—a landscape, an image—an idea that arrives on the page with a certain kind of weight and authority. It "feels true," I find. It resonates somewhere deep in the torso.

These are the moments that carry me through the early drafts. They are both signposts and nutrition. After writing for hours (days, months, years!) in the desert, I suddenly have the sense that I have not invented this thing, but that it continues on, underground and out of sight, a mystery continually demanding pursuit. And while this euphoria typically doesn't last long (less than 48 hours, most of the time) that's enough for a few key things to fall in place. A plotline gets untangled. A character takes on a new form. More importantly, I have a short-term boost of confidence. *There's a story here,* I think. *I'm not chasing after nothing.* Having caught wind of this new, truer shape, I'm driven back to the keyboard, tools in hand, ready to make something happen.

Of course, then I hit nothing but dirt and stone for months. Stories are mysterious things, and their underground veins rarely follow predictable patterns. Why should they? Would we ever want them to? But in the impatience, I'm often driven back to all the cliché neuroses. Doubt, despair, a temptation to throw the whole thing out and write something "easier" (whatever that means). It's only after months and sometimes years of these stops and starts, that I gradually begin to notice patterns in those few-and-far-between deposits of truth. I find one over here, then two further north, and suddenly, a really novel and creative connection presents itself. What if we turned this character *like this*? What if our assumed villain was actually…not?

Much of what I write here will go, or change form so dramatically it's ultimately unrecognizable, but certain passages, feelings, and ideas remain. In *Refuse to be Done*, Matt Bell calls these deposits islands, which I like for the lost-at-sea feeling being pockets of certainty. But an island never connects, and for me, an essential part of the creative act comes from discovering these two points, and then laboring—tirelessly, stubbornly—until you discover the narrative fabric that binds them together.

Let's be clear, this is *not* an efficient way of writing, but I have found it to be a beautiful one. What emerges is often surprising and weird and yet inextricably connected, something I would never have arrived at through any logical door.

(strangely, this also means one of the last things I discover in a story are the foundational elements—character goals, plot devices—as if I truly could not see the flow of my narrative until all these other, weirder pieces have fallen into my lap)

Here's the thing though: while it does sometimes feel like these ideas arrive through no volition of my own, it also only seems to happen when I'm out hunting for them. I suppose this makes a certain kind of sense. No prospector found a vein of silver in his living room. The great paradox of writing is that you can spend hours trying and failing to solve a knot in the narrative, banging your head against the keyboard, and then a solution of otherworldly elegance occurs to you in the shower. This is why I don't believe in wasted writing. Writing is both destination and vehicle, both the artifact you discover and the medium that lifts you to your most intuitive, elevated self. My first novel, *When Fire Splits the Sky,* clocks in at a trim 280 pages, and yet I wrote ten times that amount to discover it.

This is why, each day, I head out excavating with a map in hand. I study weather patterns, geological strata, the campfire stories of those who have mined this land before. But every good prospector, I imagine, eventually knows when to put the map aside and go by *feel.* And even though he's tired, knowing the odds are also slim, he also knows that someday soon he'll strike that next true vein and feel that wonderful, affirming *thrum.*

CREATING NARRATIVE ECOSYSTEMS IN FICTIONAL WORLDS

ALIA LURIA

Introduction

When a story draws me in, I often feel it is because the environment in some way participates in creating narrative momentum, as if it has taken on a life of its own, independent of the characters that move through it. For me, those worlds are essential to the success of the story. I think about them and wonder how they are developed, try to understand their interactions with the characters, and recoil when they act in ways outside of my comfort zone. A detailed and independently acting environment or ecosystem can add another layer of tension for me as well as the characters, draw me into the foreign setting and enhance my empathy with the characters navigating it. Such an ecosystem can even function as a true protagonist or antagonist. Through analysis of narratives with strong ecosystems, I seek to understand how ecosystems participate outside of simple setting of a scene, such as how an author can influence theme, plot, and characterization simply through describing the environment or ecosystem and having it act on the characters, whether physically or psychologically.

As part of my journey to understand ecosystems that have transcended their place in the general narrative to embody true forces acting upon a work of fiction, I analyzed the techniques used by certain literary speculative fiction authors like Jeff VanderMeer, Octavia E. Butler, Joseph Conrad, and J.G. Ballard. These authors have all built worlds, which I will call "narrative ecosystems" (or "ecosystems" for short) that influence characters directly or indirectly, whether by acting on them physically, mentally, through the character's own psychological transformation, or by influencing characters by serving as a means of social control imposed by other characters in the form of a sustained ecosystem. Often, it seems that these ecosystems are pushing back against a prior impact that people have made to the natural world, whether through pollution, depletion of resources, or the destructive tendencies of humanity. I will refer to these prior impacts as "triggering events."

The method of control asserted by the ecosystem does not necessarily correspond to the original impact made by the characters. The type of triggering event that spawns the formation of the ecosystem's action on the characters also does not drive the ultimate level of empathy one might feel for the characters. For example, in some of the works I discuss here, pollution and civilization has forced a responsive ecosystem totally different from what might be expected from purely scientific sources. These types of unexpected responses themselves add to the narrative quality of the ecosystems themselves. This leads me to believe that there are many different tools that we, as authors, can employ to create compelling ecosystems from a large range triggering events that coincide with the theme we are trying to express. As part of this analysis, I provide examples of naturally occurring and socially engineered narrative ecosystems and describe how the triggering event, the features of the ecosystem and the resulting impact on the characters all combine to enhance a specific theme within the work.

Ecosystems Acting Directly on Characters

Jeff VanderMeer's *Southern Reach Trilogy* is a speculative fiction series that focuses on unnamed human characters attempting to study a region of the United States only referred to in the books as Area X. The organization in the story known as Southern Reach, which has been placed in charge of researching and attempting to find a way to bring Area X back under the control of humans, has made the claims publicly that Area X is the result of an environmental event. Whether this statement is true or even believed by the Southern Reach itself is unclear even to the characters in the first instalment of the trilogy. The position that the Southern Reach takes implies that Area X itself is not a naturally occurring ecosystem but rather a direct pushback against the tampering of humanity. The trilogy slowly reveals the Southern Reach's many secrets, those which pertain to its true understanding of Area X as well as to how it has deceived its own employees. One of these secrets is that Area X itself is akin to a melding of earth and another planet. Its consciousness has not been socially engineered but does engage in social and environmental engineering of its own acting upon the Earth.

Area X is a pristine wilderness, but it has certain properties that act upon and affect the physiology and mental stability of the human characters. If Area X is truly the product of a human-caused environmental event, which, is the initial theory circulated by the Southern Reach, then it now has begun to change humanity as humanity changed it. This is an example of what appears to be a direct response to the actions of humans. I was left with the impression, after reading the first of the trilogy, *Annihilation*, that there is an alien nature or an evolutionary biology at work that heightens the consciousness of Area X. It was unclear at first, partially because the narrator, a biologist called the biologist, had a certain level of unreliability as her physiology begins to mutate due to exposure with Area X.

In the morning, I woke with my senses heightened, so that even the rough brown bark of the pines or the ordinary lunging swoop of woodpecker came to me a kind of minor revelation. The lingering fatigue from the four-day hike to the base camp had left me. Was this some side effect of the spores or just the result of a good night's sleep? I felt so refreshed that I didn't really care. (p. 37)

At first the biologist just experiences heightened senses, but this quickly transforms into being able to hear the heartbeat of a stone-capped flesh structure that the team has been exploring. Is this structure, which is referred to in the novel as the Tower, alive or does the biologist only perceive it as alive?

The third thing I noticed on the staging level before we reached the wider staircase that spiraled down, before we encountered again the words written on the wall . . . the tower was *breathing*. The tower *breathed*, and the walls when I went to touch them carried the echo of a heartbeat . . . and they were not made of stone but of *living tissue*. Those walls were still black, but a silver-white phosphorescence rose off of them. The world seemed to lurch, and I sat down heavily next to the wall, and the surveyor was by my side, trying to help me up. I don't know if I can convey the enormity of that moment in words. The tower was a living creature of some sort. *We were descending into an organism.*

"What's wrong?" the surveyor was asking me, voice muffled through her mask. "What happened?"

I grabbed her hand, forced her palm against the wall.

"Let me go!" she tried to pull away, but I kept her there.

"Do you feel that?" I asked, unrelenting. "Can you feel that?"

"Feel *what?* What are you talking about?" She was scared, of course. To her, I was acting irrationally.

Still, I persisted: "A vibration. A kind of beat." I removed my hand from hers, stepped back.

The surveyor took a long, deep breath, and kept her hand on the wall. "No. Maybe. No. No, nothing."

"What about the wall. What is it made of?"

"Stone, of course," she said. (pp. 41-2)

Is the biologist just delusional, or is Area X really alive? Prior to this scene in *Annihilation*, the biologist describes Area X as inanimate, normal earth with odd and disquieting stone structures. From this point forward, the biologist quite literally perceives her surroundings as alive, as an organism, in a way that she did not the day before.

It is unclear whether the spores she came in contact with have enhanced the biologist's perception, allowing her to see the tower for what it is, an organism, or whether the spores have only created in the biologist a sense of a living organism where none exists. Although the biologist believes she has found proof of her theory, the answer to this question is in itself irrelevant, as the effect is the same. We only experience it through her senses. Area X has come into existence as a character in and of itself. The spores in effect for the biologist are but one tool VanderMeer uses to create a sense of Area X as a cohesive character taking up arms against the human bacteria that have come to make it ill.

The cells of the psychologist, both from her unaffected shoulder and her wound, appeared to be normal human cells. So did the cells I examined from my own sample. This was impossible. I checked the samples over and over, even childishly pretending I had no interest in them before swooping down with an eagle eye.

I was convinced that when I wasn't looking at them, these cells became something else, that the very act of observation changed everything. I knew this was madness and yet still I thought it. I felt as if Area X were laughing at me then—every blade of grass, every stray insect, every drop of water. What would happen when the Crawler reached the bottom of the Tower? What would happen when it came back up?

Then I examined the samples from the village: moss from the "forehead" of one of the eruptions, splinters of wood, a dead fox, a rat. The wood was indeed wood. The rat was indeed a rat. The moss and the fox . . . were composed of modified human cells. *Where lies the strangling fruit that comes from the hand of the sinner I shall bring forth the seeds of the dead . . .* (p. 159)

Here is the biologist's purported proof that she is not merely delusional. Certain of the mosses and animals are "transformations" taking place inside Area X, like viruses and bacteria being repurposed by the human body to serve it rather than harm it. And yet this shocking revelation is by this point in the novel merely a grounding of what the biologist has perceived all along. What would be shocking to most humans is a confirmation of a pattern familiar to a biologist. Whether this is proof is in fact reliable, given that it is tailor made for the biologist and filtered through her altered senses, the environment has affected her character and changed her both physically and mentally. She believes in Area X.

Throughout the entire series, the balance of power between humanity and nature always favors Area X, and the wavering confirmation of this fact does nothing to change what has all along been a truth established by VanderMeer. Whether he speaks through Area X directly using interactions or visual perceptions with and by the biologist or indirectly through the biologist's musings about Area X or her need to anthropomorphize Area X, VanderMeer has skillfully created a character in Area X that, while unable to speak directly to the human characters, exerts its influence and power over them in ways cognizable by first the biologist and then by other characters through the remainder of the trilogy. VanderMeer successfully communicates Area X to and through the characters without ever directly anthropomorphizing the land itself or creatures residing in the area themselves. The circuitous nature of the communication, while often confusing, evokes realism in such interaction that would be lost through a direct avatar. VanderMeer creates a credible and chilling character in Area X without the use of such an avatar.

This initial mysticism dissipates by the third book, *Acceptance*, where many of the explanations are finally revealed and the references to merging and dissolving are made direct.

… because you are fading further still, fading into the landscape like a reluctant wraith, and you can hear a faint and delicate music in the distance, and something that whispered to you before is whispering again, and then you're dissolving into the wind. A kind of alien regard has twinned itself to you, easily mistaken for the atoms of the air if it did not seem somehow concentrated, purposeful. Joyful? (p. 7)

By book three, VanderMeer has directly stated that the world has combined with an alien world. Any expectations the reader may have had that this story was based on an environmental message has been completely turned on its head. There has been no evolution of our earth to fight back. It has been an encroachment all along. Still, this twist does not diminish the status of Area X as a fully developed character in the series and even serves to ease the transition of our thinking about nature as itself a potentially sentient actor.

In contrast to Jeff VanderMeer's work, J.G. Ballard's novel *The Crystal World* does not directly act to influence the characters but rather uses the same physical means of change and encroachment to indirectly impact the psyche of the humans. The novel focuses on a mysterious condition spreading from Africa, where organic matter is systematically converting to non-organic gemstone, a beautiful and hypnotic transformation that humanity first attempts to capitalize on even as it becomes clear that there is extreme danger in doing so. Ballard creates a terrifying physical transformation that captivates the characters and often makes them act outside their own interest without any direct communication or influence.

Again, it seems as if nature is fighting back and using man's innate greed against him. For, at first, the conversion of wood and leaves to intricate gemstones seems like boon to be exploited (as nature generally is). However, the process cannot be controlled, and any semblance of exploitive possibility is quickly dispensed, with humanity being displaced and overcome by the change. Ballard turns human encroachment back on people with a deep and beautiful irony. Similar to VanderMeer's trilogy, the actions of this ecosystem are deeply impactful and drive change in the behavior of the characters with a beautiful organic flow that keeps our natural world in the forefront.

At first, the environment fills people with wonder.

The forest is the most beautiful in Africa, a house of jewels. I can barely find words to describe our wonder each morning as we look out across the slopes, still half-hidden by the mist but glistening like St. Sophia, each a jeweled semi-dome. Indeed, Max says I am becoming excessively Byzantine—I wear my hair to my waist even at the clinic, and affect a melancholy expression, although in fact for the first time in many years, my heart sings! (p. 12)

The primary character, Dr. Sanders, ventures to this crystalline forest in search of his friends, who have sent a letter, indicating their wonder. The first step the change is the euphoria that seems to grip the characters, who are mesmerized by the beauty of the altered landscape. From there, the locals have seized on a way to monetize the transformation, placing objects into the path of the transformation and then retrieving them in gem form for sale.

Glittering below her in the sunlight was what appeared to be an immense crystalline orchid carved from some quartzlike mineral. The entire structure of the flower had been reproduced and then embedded within the crystal base, almost as if a living specimen had been conjured into the center of a huge cut-glass pendant. (p. 31)

Dr. Sanders is fully prepared to purchase these changed structures, which he thinks are just ornaments carved from crystal rather than actual natural objects that have been transformed. Although the locals have begun to capitalize on the environmental changes, the continued encroachment eventually turns to terror for some and compulsion for others.

"This man Radek—a captain in the medical corp—I found him in the center of the forest, completely crystallized. You know what I mean?" Max nodded, his eyes looking Sanders up and down with a more than usually watchful gaze. Sanders went on: "I thought the only way of saving him was to immerse him in the river—but I had to tear him loose! Some of the crystals came off, I didn't realize—"

"Edward!" Max took his arm and tried to steer him along the path. "There's no—"

Sanders pushed his hand away. "Max, I found him later, I'd torn half his face and chest away—!"

"For God's sake!" Max clenched his fist. "Yours wasn't the first mistake, don't reproach yourself!"

"Max, I don't—understand me, it wasn't just that!" Sanders hesitated. "The point is—he wanted to go *back*! He wanted to go back into the forest and be crystallized again! He knew, Max, he *knew*!" (p. 144)

Dr. Sanders, in the span of barely a day or two, reorients from transfixed awe to dismay at not just the transformation of the forest and physical harm that it is causing the residents, but to a certain existential horror that some of them might be so enthralled that they choose to become permanently frozen into the environment. It isn't just the ill and troubled who gravitate towards the cold immortality of the crystal forest. Dr. Radek was assisting in the evacuation when he became crystallized. Perhaps fear comes not from having harm done to the person but from recognizing the own self-destructive nature of humanity on the micro level, not just on the macro level. Self-destructive impulse is a recurring theme in *The Crystal World*. Unlike with VanderMeer's work, the ecosystem Ballard employs does not appear to have an intelligence or actively communicate or otherwise influence the humans that rush to be embedded in its ice. Its influence is borne from humanity's own inclinations toward self-destruction. Through no other method than existing as an ever-spreading status, the crystals are attributed a gravity and personality and character by the other characters in the story.

Ecosystems Impacting Characters Indirectly

Although VanderMeer and Ballard both use unsubtle physical representations for ecosystems that act on humanity, even indirectly in Ballard's case, other authors like Octavia Butler and Joseph Conrad have used both physical and psychological representations of environment to deeply affect the mental state of the characters trapped in the referenced ecosystems. The oppressiveness of these environments, which aren't derived from beauty but rather derived from force, serve to function equally effectively in driving character development, whether it's through bolstering the will of a woman trapped aboard an entirely organic transport vessel (*Dawn* by Octavia Butler) or through driving an officer to madness while trapped aboard a boat in the Amazon (*Heart of Darkness* by Joseph Conrad).

In *Dawn*, the primary character, Lilith, begins the story trapped in a room for what seems to be years. She only learns after she has been freed from it, that the room itself is made of flesh and resides on a spaceship of the alien race called the Oankali.

The hole in the wall widened as though it were flesh rippling aside, slowly writhing. She was both fascinated and repelled.

"Is it alive?" she asked

"Yes," he said.

She had beaten it, kicked it, clawed it, tried to bite it. It had been smooth, tough, impenetrable, but slightly giving like the bed and table. It had felt like plastic, cool beneath her hands.

"What is it?" she asked.

"Flesh. More like mine than yours. Different from mine, too, though. It's … the ship." (Butler, p. 29)

Lilith recalls beating the walls, not realizing it was flesh, acting out her response to the feelings of oppression. Later, although

Lilith learns to live on the ship symbiotically, as the Oankali do, feeding it her leftovers, teaching it to accomplish discrete results, she never forgets that there is no escape.

There was no escape from the ship. None at all. The Oankali controlled the ship with their own body chemistry. There were no controls that could be memorized or subverted. Even the shuttles that traveled between Earth and the ship were like extensions of Oankali bodies.

No human could do anything aboard the ship except make trouble and be put back into suspended animation—or be killed. (Butler, p. 116)

Butler creates an environment that does not in any way directly act to restrain Lilith but that manages to act as an oppressive restraint nonetheless. The ecosystem aboard the Oankali ship is a living presence, a malleable environment that simulates recognizable life while containing life unrecognizable to Lilith and the other humans. It is both a farce designed to comfort the humans and a prison designed to hold them. As much as Lilith would like to focus on the former, she cannot forget the latter, and this influences the reader's view of the ship as well, creating an ecosystem that never speaks, never acts not in direct response to a command, but which remains a psychological weight on the characters and thus the reader by extension.

Joseph Conrad, in *Heart of Darkness*, creates an entirely different kind of oppression. Conrad views the forest along the

Amazon River as a monolith that subsumes colonizers. This perhaps happens literally in the story, as the bastion of colonial Europe, Mr. Kurtz, is physically subsumed into the earth upon his death, but the psychological, rather than the physical decline, is where Conrad focuses his attention, perhaps viewing the loss of mind as more important than the loss of body.

And outside, the silent wilderness surrounding this cleared speck on the earth struck me as something great and invincible, like evil or truth, waiting patiently for the passing away of this fantastic invasion. (Conrad, p. 23)

Conrad immediately, early in the narrator's recounting of the tale, flips the setting, establishing that the forest is reality, and the pitiful excuse for colonization made by the Company is the fantastical. There is nothing supernatural about this forest. It is not made of flesh, does not invade the characters' molecules or crystalize them, but the sheer vastness of it creates an oppression just as great as if it had acted on the characters directly. Conrad is more interested in what humanity will do if left to its own imagination.

All this was great, expectant, mute, while the man jabbered about himself. I wondered whether the stillness on the face of the immensity looking at us two were meant as an appeal or as a menace. What were we who had strayed in here? Could we handle that dumb thing, or would it handle us? I felt how big, how confoundedly big, was that thing that couldn't talk, and perhaps was deaf as well. What was in there? (Conrad, pp. 26-27)

This imagery is repeated, peppered exhaustively through the opening two chapters of the novella. It is hard to fault Conrad, for this repetition, however, as the narrator is a character recounting the story in first person. It is his story. Although Conrad makes an authorial joke about the character saying the story isn't about him, but about Mr. Kurtz, he is the filter and of course injected into every aspect. Thus, it is Mr. Marlow's observation of the monolithic and oppressive quality of the forest that the reader learns about, not Conrad's.

"The earth seemed unearthly. We are accustomed to look upon the shackled form of a conquered monster, but there— there you could look at a thing monstrous and free. It was unearthly, and the men were— No, they were not inhuman. Well, you know, that was the worst of it— this suspicion of their not being inhuman. (Conrad, p. 35)

Mr. Marlow finally voices the existential worry that this great, vast living but insentient beast of an earth has unleashed on his psyche—the fear that maybe what man becomes in the wild is really "humanity" and that the measure of humanity can only be gauged truly against this monster in the wild, not against the farce of the beast conquered. It is a question that Mr. Marlow still grapples with many years later, as he is urged by some unknown force to recount this story to his friends and colleagues. Conrad uses nothing but raw nature to drive its character development toward some idea or mental resolution, to question their own humanity.

But the wilderness had found him out early, and had taken on him a terrible vengeance for the fantastic invasion. I think it had whispered to him things about himself which he did not know, things of which he had no conception till he took counsel with this great solitude— and the whisper had proved irresistibly fascinating. It echoed loudly within him because he was hollow at the core . . . (Conrad, p. 55)

This sentiment is reiterated with particular focus on Mr. Kurtz and his descent into madness. The idea of the body existing without the mind is the ultimate existential horror for Mr. Marlow. To look inside himself and find nothing of substance, an existence as empty as the forest. Of course, the forest is not empty. It is an unchecked mass of life. It has taken in and broken down the unmitigated genius of Mr. Kurtz. The genius of "civilization" cannot stand against the monolith.

Conclusion

Through stoic and inert environs, both Butler and Conrad create differing yet equally powerful feelings of oppression.

These powerful representations of ecosystems are primary drivers of the character development in both novels. VanderMeer and Ballard instead impose actively their environments on the characters. The ecosystems of VanderMeer and Ballard modify the characters in their novels directly, through the mutagenic properties of Area X and through a crystallization process, which in turn indirectly affects the psychological states of the characters in ways that appear to alter their perception. VanderMeer and Ballard create ecosystems that, in the most direct sense, fight back. They act on humans by imposing themselves on the physical structure of the characters and subvert them through this change.

Butler and Conrad take a subtler approach in their novels. Their ecosystems oppress psychologically just by existing as painted by the authors, but the static nature of these ecosystems in no way diminishes the authors' ability to drive narrative momentum. Butler and Conrad depict characters who move through the story impacted by these ecosystems even as the ecosystems remain the same. Particularly, these novels convey feelings of oppression or entrapment, a certain hopelessness that any amount of individual power will dominate the characters' surroundings. In the case of Conrad, this vastness is even capable of swallowing a way of life rather than just containing it.

Whether these are examinations of what it means to be human, what it means to exist in an environment, ecological warnings, or even what it means to confront an alien force, these authors create narrative momentum through their environments, not just tell a story located within in such environments. The environments themselves are a character in the story or even the story itself.

SET TO FALL

JOSH RANK

Playing things too safe is the most popular way to fail. —Elliott Smith

I've never broken up with anybody. In a circular way, I think this ultimately comes from a fear of rejection. Though I'd be rejecting somebody else, it would lead me to a position where I would have to put myself back out there and potentially be rejected myself. Rejection hurts. Nobody wants to look another person in the eyes and be told you're not good enough, smart enough, fast enough. And each time it happens, you lose another piece of yourself.

Who would volunteer for this type of abuse?

It takes a special kind of freak to want to be a writer. First, there's the egocentric belief that your thoughts are so precious that they must be put to paper, solidified into posterity so they can be studied for centuries. Second, there's the masochistic urge to not only put your thoughts, feelings, and emotions out there for others to see, but judged.

A layer of separation exists between the office and the reading world. It's a mechanism called publishing and it can either be your white whale or your best friend. But even those on the friendly side of publishing had to climb an ice-covered mountain to get there. And all the way up, invisible arrows are shot from unseen places that strike you directly in the heart over and over and over.

The dirty secret of the writer's life is that figuring out how to push syllables and descriptors around the page is only the first half of the battle. After years of putting together your prized manuscript that lays bare every fear and hidden thought, you must put it in the sunlight for passersby to glance at briefly and say, "Hmm, not good enough."

And the only thing you can do is say thank you, pull the arrow from your chest, and do it all over again.

Of course, this process is necessary. As a reader, how could you possibly find the next great book if the market was flooded with every book ever written? There would be a continent of material to wade through and the casual reader would simply give up and sit in front of the television until they died. There needs to be a culling. A filter. Of course *you* love your writing, but that doesn't mean it's objectively good.

It's very easy to think you've written something awesome when it, in fact, sucks. Take it from me—I do it all the time. I wrote five novels before getting one published. There was absolutely zero difference between the way I felt about each book upon completion. I was convinced they were all publishable. I was wrong.

People who play guitar build up calluses on their fingertips over time. Marathon runners grow stronger over years of training. And writers grow a protective layer of armor around their hearts from years of rejection. Those that don't, perish.

There's no way to practice for rejection. There's no shortcut or way to condition yourself besides simply accepting it and letting it wash over you. If at all possible, make a joke out of it. Rejection is inevitable and simply a part of life like traffic jams and colonoscopies.

After thousands of rejections, it's funny to look back at my very first letter from the *Chicago Review*. This was long enough ago that it was an actual rejection letter, on paper, sent through the mail, and carried by a mail carrier. I was excited. It felt like a welcome into the world of writers and even though it was a rejection, it also felt like a validation.

You are in the game. You are part of the literary world.

It was invigorating, but of course that wore off. It would be another three years until I finally placed my first short story in a magazine. I once read that Fiona Apple didn't think she enjoyed or appreciated her early success because it seemed so simple. She played music, a record executive liked it, so they put out an album and it became wildly popular. She didn't go through years of eating rejections until something finally broke through.

So while of course it would have been much easier to get an acceptance from the very beginning, that ride into work the morning I received that email from the *Feathertale Review* was exuberant because after years of trying, the email didn't start with the word, "While."

You. Reader. You are likely a writer. Stephen King told us that writing is telepathy. And as always, he's exactly right. How else could the words I'm thinking as I write this enter your brain as you read this? We need to be careful how we wield this power. Kurt Vonnegut gave us a great edict to direct our writing efforts: "Use the time of a total stranger in such a way that he or she will not feel the time was wasted."

At the same time, it's important to not feel like you're wasting your own time. And it can feel like that when every Submittable email brings a degree of pain. Why put yourself through this? Why try in the first place?

I can only speak for myself here, and my answer is that I don't know. It's simply something I like to do even though I know I'm going to be told I'm not good enough (or not a good fit) a thousand more times before my eyes finally fall out of my head. And that's okay. Because realistically, publishing is not the goal. Rejections only have total power over you if seeing your name in print is the big payoff. And if that's the case, you should just write a letter to the editor of your local paper and get it over with. The goal is exploration, illumination, and—let's just say it—fucking around.

Some people fuck around with trainspotting, others with puppetry, and others with soap sculpting. We fuck around with words. The power of rejection will only feel real if you lose sight of that.

ABOUT THE AUTHORS

BROOK BHAGAT

Brook Bhagat (she/her) is the author of *Only Flying*, a Pushcart-nominated collection of surreal poetry and flash fiction on paradox, rebellion, transformation, and enlightenment from Unsolicited Press. Her work has won contests and appeared in *Monkeybicycle, Empty Mirror, Soundings East, Anthem: A Tribute to Leonard Cohen,* and other journals and anthologies. She is a founding editor of *Blue Planet Journal* and a professor of creative writing at Pikes Peak State College, and she facilitates workshops and other literary events. Read her newest work and contact her through https://brook-bhagat.com/, and follow her on social media @BrookBhagat.

TAYLOR GARCÍA

Taylor García is the author of the novel *Slip Soul,* the short story collection *Functional Families,* and several short stories and essays. He also writes the weekly column, "Father Time" at the Good Men Project, and holds an MFA from Pacific University Oregon. García is a multi-generational Neomexicano originally from Santa Fé, New Mexico now living in Southern California with his wife and children.

JENNIFER CLARK

Jennifer Clark lives and writes in Kalamazoo, Michigan. Her latest book, *Kissing the World Goodbye* (Unsolicited Press), ventures into the world of memoir, braiding family tales with recipes. Her fourth poetry collection, *Saints for Concerning Occasions*, is due out May 2025 from Unsolicited Press. Find her at jenniferclarkkzoo.com and @jenniferclarkbooks.

KELLI ALLEN

Kelli Allen's work has appeared in numerous journals and anthologies in the US and internationally. Allen is the co-Founding Editor of *Book of Matches* literary journal. Allen's latest book is *Leaving the Skin on the Bear*, C&R Press, 2022. She currently teaches writing and literature in North Carolina. www.kelli-allen.com

ANDY SMART

Andy Smart earned his MFA in Creative Nonfiction from the Solstice Creative Writing Program at Lasell University, where he was a Michael Steinberg Fellow. Andy's essays have appeared in *Salamander, Sleet Magazine,* and *Moon City Review* as well the anthologies *Show Me All Your Scars* (In Fact Books) and *Come Shining: Essays and Poems on Writing in a Dark Time* (Kelson Books). His poetry has appeared in *Lily Poetry Review, The American Journal of Poetry,* and elsewhere. Andy was a 2019

Pushcart Prize nominee. His first chapbook of hybrid poetry, *Blue Horse Suite*, is available from Kattywompus Press. This is his first book. Andy lives in Missouri and online at www.AndySmartWrites.com.

JOHN BISCELLO

John Biscello is the author of four novels, two poetry collections, and two children's books. The Bride, a short film he wrote and directed, debuted in 2024. His novel, No One Dreams in Color, will be published by Unsolicted Press (Spring 2026).

Website/blog: johnbiscello.com
Instagram: @johnbiscello

LINDA CARADINE

Linda Caradine is a writer, traveler and animal lover. Her memoir, Lying Down with Dogs, is available at www.unsolicited press.com and on Amazon. You can reach Linda at http://www.LindaCaradine.com."

DAVID NASH

David Nash is an author, singer songwriter, father and husband, who regularly suffers from imposter syndrome. He lives in Minnesota where he is irrationally optimistic about the cold.

You can follow him on instagram at @nash_david_ and find all of his works at davidnashcollective.com

MICK BENNETT

Mick Bennett grew up in Belmar, New Jersey. He is married and lives with his wife of forty-one years, Kathleen, and Jovie, their golden retriever. Set him before an ocean, and he will love you.

mickbennettnj.com

X:michaelbennet29

IG:mickbennettauthor

TYLER JAMES RUSSELL

Tyler James Russell is the author of *When Fire Splits the Sky* ("the most riveting, original book I've read in ages," said Laura Davis), a novel, and *To Drown a Man*, a poetry collection, both from Unsolicited Press. He works as a teacher and lives in Pennsylvania with his wife Cat and their children. His writing has been nominated for the Rhysling and Best of the Net, and has appeared in *Asimov's Science Fiction*, *F(r)iction*, and the *Hoxie Gorge Review*, among others. You can find him (sporadically) at Tylerjamesrussell.com, on Twitter/X at @TJamesRussell, or on Instagram @_TJamesRussell.

ALIA LURIA

Alia Luria is a novelist and essayist. She received her MFA in Fiction from Fairleigh Dickinson University. Her first full-length collection of essays will be published by Unsolicited Press in 2025. Visit https://www.stillnotarobot.com for more thoughts on the craft of writing.

Alia Luria's debut novel, *Compendium*, was published in 2014 and received the National Indie Excellence Award in Fantasy, the Reader's Favorite Silver Medal in Fantasy, and was a finalist for the Independent Author Network Book of the Year Award in three categories, including First Novel. The second novel in the series, *Ocularum*, is forthcoming. Her personal essay, "You Might Eat Organic, but You're Full of Baloney," was a creative nonfiction finalist for the Malahat Review Open Season Awards in 2018 and was published by *Northwest Review*. Her work has also appeared in *Toho Journal* and *Wingless Dreamer*.

JOSH RANK

Josh Rank lives, works, shops, and naps in Appleton, Wisconsin. Learn more about his dogs and his books at www.joshrank.com.

* 9 7 8 1 9 6 3 1 1 5 3 6 9 *